The
Salem
Witch
Trials

How History Is Invented

The Salem Witch Trials

Lori Lee Wilson

Lerner Publications Company
Minneapolis

Dedicated to Betty, Jenni, Michael, Philip, Tim-Edward, and Thomas

A special thank you to Don and Liz Hunt for all their help

Library of Congress Cataloging-in-Publication Data

Wilson, Lori Lee.
    The Salem witch trials / Lori Lee Wilson.
    p.   cm. — (How history is invented)
    Includes bibliographical references and index.
    Summary: Discusses the witchcraft trials in Salem in 1692, the events leading up to them, and how the trials have been viewed by different historians since then.
    ISBN 0-8225-4889-5 (alk. paper)
    1. Witchcraft—Massachusetts—Salem—History—Juvenile literature. 2. Trials (Witchcraft)—Massachusetts—Salem—Juvenile literature. 3. Salem (Mass.)—History—Juvenile literature. 4. Salem (Mass.)—Social conditions—Juvenile literature. [1. Witchcraft—Massachusetts—Salem. 2. Trials (Witchcraft)—Massachusetts—Salem.] I. Title. II. Series.
BF1575.N612 1997
133.4'3'097445—dc20   96-21371

Manufactured in the United States of America
1 2 3 4 5 6 – JR – 02 01 00 99 98 97

CONTENTS

—⁓ ✝ ⁓—

This undated woodcut shows the final ingredient being added to the witches' brew.

—❧ ONE ❧—

THE EVOLUTION OF WITCHCRAFT

"Strange and contradictory Notions have always prevailed regarding the Being, Powers and Agencies of Witches."
—Samuel Drake, *Annals of Witchcraft*

THE WORD *WITCH* COMES FROM THE CELTIC WORD *wicca*, meaning "wise one" or "magician." A witch is a person believed to have received special powers. From earliest times, people in all parts of the world have believed in witches. According to some scholars, more than half the people in the world still think witches can influence their lives.

Witchcraft is the use of supposedly magical powers, generally to harm people or damage their property. Witchcraft as practiced in European countries has differed from witchcraft elsewhere. European witchcraft is anti-Christian and involves an association with the devil. A witch might sell his or her soul to the devil in exchange for magic powers. Witchcraft in Africa and the West Indies and among the Indians of North America does not involve the devil. Such non-European witchcraft usually is used to harm people, but it can also help people. For example, someone in love might want a love potion to give to the loved one. Drinking the potion will supposedly make the loved one return the giver's love.

To find out about witches and witchcraft, historians have dug up answers older than written history. At Lascaux, France, archaeologists found a cave with charcoal drawings dating back to 35,000 B.C. They also found amber amulets at burial sites in the cave. An amulet is a necklace bearing the image or symbol of a spirit. The person wearing the amulet may have believed it would shield him or her from harm. Archaeologists also found corpses bound with cords. The skulls from the corpses look like they might have been used as receptacles for drinking.

These clues strongly suggest that Stone Age people believed that spirits of the dead lingered on earth and were capable of hurting or helping the living. Perhaps the dead were bound so they could do no harm. Perhaps skulls were used as vessels so the living could drink the spirits' wisdom. Some archaeologists think the paintings on the walls at Lascaux may even have been a form of witchcraft. By creating images of wild beasts, the cave dwellers may have hoped to give their hunters power over the spirits of animals. There are also paintings of a pregnant, large-breasted woman, possibly representing the

This Zulu witch doctor had to go through an apprenticeship to learn his skills. Witches supposedly inherit their skills.

nurturing goddess of fertility. Images of fertility goddesses have been found at excavation sites all over the world. The idea of a fertility goddess has been and continues to be intertwined with that of the witch.

Anthropologists studying primitive cultures have found many similarities between tribal and prehistoric beliefs. In some places, witch doctors still perform spirit-binding burial rites and prescribe amulets as protection against harm. When there is a drought, sickness, or some other misfortune, people in primitive societies often blame evil spirits or the local witch. Witchcraft exists among the Hopi and Navajo Indians of the southwestern United States, the Maori of New Zealand, and many peoples in southern Africa. In the West Indies, the beliefs and practices of voodoo are very similar to those of witchcraft. A witch, in some societies, is an old woman—often a widow—who lives alone, usually outside the village. She is believed to have inherited her magic powers from a parent—unlike a witch doctor, who must go through an apprenticeship to learn his or her craft.

People who believe in witches think a witch can harm people in various ways. Witches may use ceremonial music, dancing, and incantations. Sometimes a witch casts a spell by reciting a magic formula. The spell makes the victim suffer. Witches also use masks or dolls to create the likeness of spirits and people. For example, a witch might make a small wax or wooden image of the victim. She might put something from the victim's body, such as fingernail clippings or hair, into the image. Then the witch destroys the image by cutting it, burning it, or sticking pins into it. The victim supposedly suffers severe pain or death.

Witches are said to mark the movement of the sun, moon, and stars and relate that movement to life and events on earth. They might also make animal sacrifices and concoct medicines, poisons, or hallucinogens from minerals, herbs, fungi, roots, insects, and small reptiles.

Witches in Fairy Tales

Witches are often found in fairy tales. Although these stories take place in an unreal world inhabited by imaginary characters, many people still criticize the tales for being frightening, violent, and immoral.

In the fairy tale Hansel and Gretel, *the witch casts her spell over Gretel. Hansel stands helpless in the cage behind the witch.*

In *Hansel and Gretel,* by the German writers Jakob Grimm and Wilhelm Grimm, the witch is a wicked old woman who built a house of bread, cake, and sugar candy to lure children inside. When a child came into her power, she would kill it, cook it, and eat it. According to the story, "witches have red eyes and can't see far, but they have a keen sense of smell, like animals, so that they can tell whenever human beings get near." Gretel outsmarts the witch and pushes her into the oven, where she burns to death. After the witch has been killed, the children find pearls and precious stones. They return to their father's house and live in "perfect happiness."

In the story of *Rapunzel,* also by the brothers Grimm, there is "a witch of great might, and of whom the whole world was afraid." She kept the beautiful, young Rapunzel in a tower without stairs or a door. When the witch, called Mother Gothel, learned about Rapunzel's visits from the king's son, she banished Rapunzel and put a curse on her lover. "Aha!" cried the witch. "You came for your darling, but the sweet bird sits no longer in the nest, and sings no more; the cat has got her, and will scratch out your eyes as well! Rapunzel is lost to you; you will see her no more." The king's son jumps from the tower but is blinded by thorns when he lands. Good overcomes evil, however. After searching in blindness for years, his sight is restored when he finds Rapunzel and her tears fall on his eyes.

In the Russian tale *Vasilissa the Fair*, Baba Yaga is a witch who eats people. The fence around her house is made of dead people's bones. Human skulls with glowing eyes in them sit on top of the fence. Baba Yaga rides "in a mortar, urging it on with a pestle, sweeping away her traces with a broom." She has special powers that can part walls and open gates. The glowing eyes in the skull that she sends home with Vasilissa, the fair young maiden, burn the wicked stepmother and stepsisters. Rather than eat Vasilissa, the witch releases her because the girl had been blessed by her mother years before, when the mother lay dying. Baba Yaga says, "Get along out of my house, you bless'd daughter. I don't want bless'd people."

In all these fairy tales, good wins out over evil, but all the witches have supernatural powers and are associated with evil.

Witches and the Devil

Fairy-tale witches may be associated with evil, but how did the devil become associated with witches and witchcraft? The answer has proved elusive. In trying to find the link, historians have had to trace the history of the devil. Where did the idea of a devil come from? The history of the devil does not reach back as far as the concept of witchcraft, although fear of evil spirits is at least as old. In some cultures, including that of the Algonquian and Iroquois, two Native American tribes, creation myths tell of an evil twin of the Good Spirit. But the concept of the devil came out of ancient Jewish tradition, dating roughly to 1500 B.C. The word *satan* comes from the Hebrew word for *adversary*. When Hebrew scriptures were translated into Greek, the word *diabolos*, meaning slanderer, was used to indicate Satan. The English word *devil* was derived from *diabolos*. The word *satan* originally meant any sort of adversary, whether human, beast, or

The devil has been depicted in various forms. The engraving on the left shows him with batlike wings and serpents beside him. In the center, he is being banished from heaven to hell for rebelling against God. To the right, he is represented with a triple face, devouring three bodies.

angel. Later, it came to mean adversary of God, the fallen angel named Lucifer, who—with his followers—was hurled from heaven to hell because of his revolt against God. Lucifer also became known as Satan and the devil.

In Hebrew and Christian scripture, Satan's name began to be used interchangeably with that of the Babylonian god, Beelzebub. Literally, *Beelzebub* means "lord of the flies." In ancient Babylon (2200 B.C.–200 B.C.), Beelzebub was a horned god, master of plagues and ruler of the dead. His priests were wizards and necromancers—people who claimed they could communicate with the spirits of the dead to reveal the future or influence the course of events.

The image of the devil also merged with that of Pan, the god of pastures in Greek mythology. The ancient Greeks believed Pan had a wild, unpredictable nature. They also thought he had the power to fill human beings and animals with sudden, unreasoning terror. Pan is often depicted as a grimacing goat-man with horns, cloven hooves, and a tail. Satan is also portrayed that way in both early and medieval Christian art. The Greek word *demon* was also applied to the devil and his followers. Demons, in Greek mythology, were evil spirits who could take possession of a person's mind and body, causing him or her to rave, foam at the mouth, fall into fits, blurt prophecies and hidden truths, or fall madly in love. Many religious groups had exorcists, people who used prayers and incantations to cast out demons.

The most famous enchantress in ancient Greek mythology is Medea. Like the primitive witch, Medea is said to have inherited her magical powers. Unlike the witch, Medea was young, beautiful, and the daughter of a king. According to the myth, Medea helped the hero Jason capture the Golden Fleece, the famous golden wool of a flying ram. Jason and Medea had two sons and lived happily for 10 years. Then Jason fell in love with Glauke, the daughter of another king. He abandoned Medea to marry Glauke. Medea took revenge by using magic to burn the bride. Medea then murdered her sons with a knife, so Jason would have no heirs.

Medea served the sorceress Circe, who could turn men into beasts, and the goddess Hecate, who was usually associated with the underworld and witchcraft. Hecate was a goddess of the night and was associated with the moon. People believed she appeared at crossroads, where the spirits of those about to be born would enter the world and the spirits of those about to die would depart from the world. The Greek goddess Artemis and the Roman goddess Diana were related

 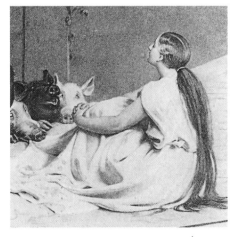

The goddess Medea, on the left, is pictured murdering her sons with a knife. On the right, the enchantress Circe has changed men into swine.

Hecate, goddess of the underworld, is shown on the left. An ancient sculpture of the goddess Diana is pictured on the right.

to the nurturing goddess of fertility. Hecate, Artemis, and Diana are all associated with witches and witchcraft.

Some scholars think witchcraft is an extremely old system of organized religious worship. In many parts of Europe, peasants engaged in secret rituals associated with Hecate and Diana. According to historian Montague Summers, people sometimes sacrificed small animals, taking the creatures to a crossroads at night and tearing them to pieces. Those who were caught by church officials were charged with witchcraft and told that they served the devil in performing such rites. The same thing was said to those who were caught worshipping Diana. Her worshippers gathered in wooded glens on moonlit nights. They feasted on cakes and wine, then stripped naked and engaged in wild singing and dancing that generally ended in a drunken orgy. By doing this, they were giving their bodies to the devil, church leaders warned. To discourage such behavior, those who were caught were imprisoned or burned at the stake. Hecate, Diana, witchcraft, and the devil had become inseparable.

From the 1400s to the 1700s, church authorities in Europe tried to eliminate witchcraft. Church persecution of witches took place in England, France, Germany, Italy, Scotland, and Spain. In 1431 the

English accused the French national heroine Joan of Arc of being a witch. She was condemned to death and burned at the stake. According to some historians, the Christian church put to death about 300,000 women for practicing witchcraft between 1484 and 1782. Many women were so severely tortured that they confessed to being witches to avoid further torment.

Bishops, ministers, and courtroom justices were the authors of virtually all books and articles about witchcraft written between 1400 and 1700. Drawing on their own witch-hunting experiences, these writers offered definitions of witchcraft, methods of discovering whether a suspect was a witch, ways to get a witch to confess, and methods to punish the guilty. People who practiced "white magic"—the use of good luck charms or love ointments—were mildly punished, if they were punished at all. Those who practiced "black magic" with the intent to hurt or kill, whether successful or not, were executed. And those who were considered most dangerous—those who sold their souls to the devil, worshipped him, and had from him the power to cause storms, plague, war, and famine—were burned at the stake.

During the 1600s and 1700s, an almost hysterical fear of witchcraft swept through most of Europe. During this time, the courts allowed gossip and rumor to be used as evidence, and many children testified against their own parents. The American colonists brought their belief in witchcraft from England to the New World.

The Puritan family depicted here is based on an 1876 painting by American artist George H. Boughton.

⌐⌐ TWO ⌐⌐

SALEM WITCHCRAFT

*"We shall be as a City upon a Hill, the eyes of all People
are upon us; so that if we shall deal falsely with our God in
this work we have undertaken, and so cause him to withdraw his present help from us, we shall be made a by-word
through the world."*

—John Winthrop

N 1692 THE MASSACHUSETTS BAY COLONY WAS AN isolated but growing Puritan community in the North American wilderness. The population was scattered. Villages and farms outside the seaport towns of Boston and Salem were separated by a half-day's travel or more. Communication and travel were slow, since most people walked. Settlers in isolated communities like Salem Village often felt threatened by the presence of bears and other wild animals and by attacks from Native Americans. The colonists frequently mistrusted each other and quarreled about issues such as land boundaries. One family filed a lawsuit after a neighbor's pig got into its vegetable garden and ate much of the winter food supply.

The spiritual life of Puritans who lived in isolated areas like Salem Village may have added to their sense of vulnerability. Puritan doctrine stressed that everything was in God's hands. Good fortune and health came to those whom God blessed. Salvation was a gift from God. In worship services, Puritans emphasized Bible reading, prayer, and preaching, and they believed in grace, devotion, prayer, and self-examination to achieve religious virtue.

Tituba, later accused of witchcraft, is entertaining the children.

The Puritans also believed that God allowed Satan to tempt and torment those who strayed from the path of righteousness and acted immorally or those whose faith God wanted to test. These people suffered misfortune, sickness and grief. Satan might also come into a person's life in the form of a witch. Puritans attributed almost all actions to the mystical powers of God or Satan.

The Salem Village witchcraft drama began in mid-January 1692 at the home of the Reverend Samuel Parris. Because he didn't complete his schooling at Harvard, Parris had had to settle for a position in the little-known parish of Salem Village, later renamed Danvers. Northwest of the more established and bustling seaport town of Salem, Salem Village was considered to be a backcountry hamlet. The Parris house was cold, and there was not enough firewood. Added to this, Samuel Parris had just learned that he would not be receiving his salary for a while. The minister's bitterness over this situation came out in his sermons and affected life at his home as well.

Perhaps hoping for a brighter future, 9-year-old Betty Parris and her cousin, 11-year-old Abigail Williams, who lived with the Parris family, played with white magic. So did other girls in the neighborhood, most of whom were in their teens. Using a "Venus glass" (a mirror) and an egg, the girls tried to predict the occupations their hoped-for husbands might have. The girls set an uncooked, unbroken egg spinning in the middle of a mirror, stopped it with a touch of a finger, and then released it. As soon as it was released, the egg began to spin again, as if by magic. By staring at a spinning egg under the dim light of a candle, the girls hoped to see into the future. One or two of them thought they saw a casket—a terrifying vision that clouded the harmless white magic.

Before coming to Salem Village, Samuel Parris had been a merchant in Barbados, an island in the Caribbean. When he and his family moved in 1689, he brought a West Indian slave called Tituba, her husband, John Indian, and one or more other slaves. Although there is no evidence, historians suspect that Tituba entertained the children with Caribbean fables. Certainly Betty's mother would have told the girls English fairy tales—partly to entertain and partly to instruct— since the tales had morals to them. Both of these storytelling traditions speak of magic and good and evil spirits.

People in the early colonies often walked to church in groups for protection. The men carried muskets to ward off possible attacks by Indians. This 1867 painting is by George H. Boughton.

The Puritans

In 1629 King Charles I of England granted a charter (a set of laws) to a religious group called the Puritans. The charter gave the Puritans the right to settle and govern an English colony in the Massachusetts Bay area of North America. In 1630 John Winthrop, a lawyer and country gentleman, led about one thousand English colonists to Massachusetts Bay.

The Church of England had been established a century before John Winthrop and the other colonists arrived at Massachusetts Bay. In 1531, King Henry VIII had the English Parliament declare that the king—not the Catholic pope—was the head of the church in England. These actions took place while a religious movement called the Reformation was spreading across northern Europe. The Reformation led to the beginning of Protestantism, the term used for hundreds of Christian denominations. In the decade that followed, many reforms occurred in the Church of England. The Puritans, who had originally been part of the Church of England, encouraged reform. They rejected Catholic traditions and wanted to "purify" the church. That is why they were called Puritans.

The English king took a more moderate view, and many Catholic traditions remained in the Church of England. The dissatisfied Puritans then formed churches of their own. They objected to frills, such as fancy lace collars and feathered hats. They also denounced popular pastimes, such as the maypole dance. The term *Puritan* was soon used to refer to those thought to be intolerant, self-righteous bigots. People also noticed that Puritans thought working hard to gain wealth—even at the expense of their neighbors—was a good thing. To the Puritans, wealth meant that God had blessed them. But to non-Puritans, the plainly clothed but wealthy Puritan seemed to be a hypocrite. As it became more difficult to practice their religious beliefs in England, many Puritans moved to the New World, seeking religious freedom. By 1640 the Massachusetts Bay Colony had about 10,000 settlers. Many Puritans settled in the area of present-day Boston. This area included the towns of Salem and Salem Village.

The colonists built churches, where they gathered to sing hymns, pray, and receive moral instruction. Their churches, however, were not only places of worship. They were also the seat of Puritan colonial government. Ministers and magistrates— public officials with administrative and judicial functions—governed their communities. At church, men gathered to vote, elect officials, debate laws, write charters, and consider evidence when disputes arose. In the1600s, there was little separation between church and state. For example, the magistrates passed a law requiring all colonists to join a church congregation. Men who did not join a congregation gave up their right to vote. The Bible served not only as a source for religious instruction, but also as a legal guide. The Puritans organized their government in the New World according to the Bible and on the basis of their English experience. They believed they were God's "elect," his chosen people, who would dwell with him in heaven. Those who were not part of the elect would be cast into hell, as Lucifer had been.

The Puritans living at Massachusetts Bay Colony faced many difficulties, such as crop failure, hunger, cold, war, and attacks from wild animals and hostile Native Americans, whose land the colonists had taken. The Puritans found strength in their faith, but at times that faith was shaken. They did not coexist as peacefully as they had hoped. While some prospered, others did not. Property disputes arose. People accused each other of crimes and immoral behavior. Religious differences developed as new colonists arrived.

Puritan ministers warned that God would "withdraw his present help" if people continued to "deal falsely with God" and with each other. Although the Puritans believed they were God's elect, they also believed they could lose God's favor if they failed to lead pure and upright lives. They wanted to purify themselves and their communities, which led them to weed out people they considered witches. The Puritans thought witches were guided by the devil, and they did not want the devil in their midst. During one such purification process—in Salem Village in 1692—19 people were hanged on Gallows Hill and one man, Giles Corey, was "press'd to death" under a pile of fieldstone. Their alleged crime: witchcraft.

The Reverend Samuel Parris also instructed the children. He taught them their catechism and led the whole household in daily prayer. On Sundays the family went to church and spent long hours singing hymns and listening to Samuel preach. His sermons were spiced with biting reminders of what was in store for sinners. He said that only God's elect would go to heaven.

Although no one knows why, one day in February 1692, Betty Parris and Abigail Williams began slipping into trances, cowering in corners, blurting nonsensical phrases, and—worst of all—collapsing into shrieking epilepticlike fits. Their bodies supposedly twisted as though their bones were made of putty. What is worse, the behavior spread. Twelve-year-old Ann Putnam Jr. and 19-year-old Mercy Lewis, a maidservant in Ann Putnam's household, began to suffer the same sort of fits. Then 16-year-old Mary Walcott, 18-year-old Susannah Sheldon, 16-year-old Elizabeth Booth, and 20-year-old Mary Warren exhibited the same behavior.

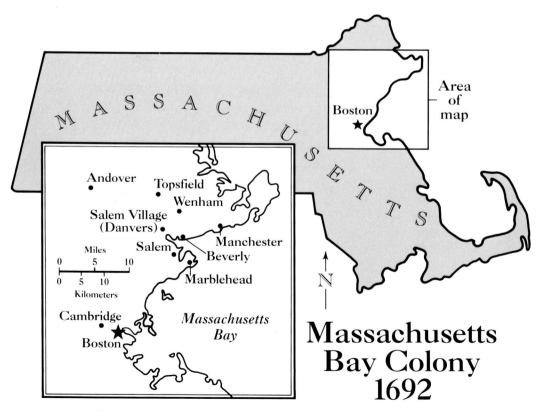

Massachusetts
Bay Colony
1692

Samuel Parris invited several doctors to examine the children, but none knew what to make of the situation. Finally, Dr. William Griggs, who thought at first that the affliction might be epilepsy, diagnosed witchcraft. He probably decided on this diagnosis because the symptoms resembled those described in the Reverend Cotton Mather's book *Memorable Providences Relating to Witchcraft and Possession.* Not long after giving this diagnosis, Dr. Griggs's maidservant, 17-year-old Betty Hubbard, began to suffer the same frightening symptoms.

In his book about witchcraft, printed in 1689 and widely read, Cotton Mather described how he had successfully cured the affliction of witchcraft by praying and fasting. The Reverend Parris now employed the same method. He invited the entire congregation to pray and fast. He summoned church deacons and other leading churchmen to his home to pray in unison. They prayed for weeks, but the girls still thrashed and shrieked and babbled nonsense. After their fits, they appeared rosy-cheeked and calm. Asked what or who had caused them to suffer so, they could not answer.

Because the cure was not working, the Reverend Parris decided to invite neighboring ministers to pray with him. Nathaniel Noyes, John Hale, John Higginson Sr., and Deodat Lawson, who had preceded Parris as minister in Salem Village, were among the ministers who came. Though they fasted and prayed long hours for several days, the ministers saw no improvement in the girls. Nonetheless, they recommended that Parris continue along the same course and keep the matter quiet lest the community make too much of it.

Samuel Parris did as they advised—until Mary Sibley, a member of his church, gave Tituba and John Indian an old English recipe for witch cake. Sibley said the cake would help them discover who the witch was. John Indian accordingly collected the children's urine, mixed it with rye, and gave it to Tituba to bake in ashes. She then fed the concoction to the household dog. According to old English superstition, all dogs are familiar with the devil. Supposedly, after eating the cake, the dog would run to the witch, who was the devil's agent. Apparently, the cake only made the dog sick.

The Reverend Parris found out about the witch cake and scolded Mary Sibley in front of the whole congregation for "going to the devil for help against the devil." She had to stand and publicly repent. She did so with many tears and was never accused of witchcraft again.

In mid-February, the Reverend Parris called for a Day of Humiliation, on which the whole congregation was to fast and pray. Meanwhile, Parris urged the girls to tell him who the witches were. They named Tituba, probably because she was the one who baked the witch cake. Unsatisfied, Parris and visiting minister John Hale continued to question the girls. Eventually they also named Sarah Good and Sarah Osborne, two village women.

On February 28, Samuel Parris wrote a letter to magistrates John Hathorne and Jonathan Corwin of Salem. Ann Putnam Jr.'s father, Thomas, delivered the letter. The following day, March 1, 1692, Tituba Indian, Sarah Good, and Sarah Osborne were charged with witchcraft and arrested. Authorities brought the three women to Ingersoll Inn for questioning, but when the magistrates arrived, they found a great crowd of spectators gathered outside. They decided to

Samuel Parris, who was instrumental in the 1692 trials, was the minister in Salem Village

move the proceedings into the church—also called the meeting-house—where there was room enough to accommodate everyone.

Sarah Good was questioned first. A pregnant, weathered woman of 38, she said she did not go to church because she did not own any clothes decent enough to wear to the worship service. Good was known to go door-to-door, begging for food and tobacco. The magistrates asked what it was she muttered to herself when she left a house. "My psalms," she said. "I hope I may say my psalms." But she was unable to remember her psalms in front of the magistrates.

Sarah Osborne was a sick, elderly woman. She had not attended church for more than a year, in part because of illness, in part because of gossip. Many years earlier, after her husband died, she had permitted her manservant to live with her in her house. She later married him, but that did not stop people from talking about her "sin." Osborne was amazed at the suffering of the afflicted girls but insisted she was innocent and knew nothing about witchcraft.

Tituba was the last to be questioned. At first, she said she knew nothing and could not explain what caused the children to suffer. According to court records, Magistrate Hathorne then asked her, "What is it that hurts them?"

"The devil for ought I know," she replied.

"How doeth he appear when he hurts them?" he asked. "With what shape? What is he like that hurts them?"

"Like a man, I think."

From that point on, her interrogation became a confession. She mentioned four other witches, Good, Osborne, and two she did not know. She spoke of a tall man from Boston and of witches' Sabbaths. Tituba described the devil as "a tall man with black clothes," a man who could change shape. Sometimes he appeared as "a great black dog," or as a hog, or as black and red rats. He had a yellow bird that he suckled, and he carried a book that he urged her to sign. He promised to give her "pretty things" if she served him, then threatened to hurt her when she refused. She had met with him in Boston, she said, and at other times in the woods. There were other witches too, she claimed. They rode through the night on sticks. They went

An elderly woman is arrested for practicing witchcraft.

to the children and pinched them, bit them, and tried to kill them.

To the magistrates and village leaders, the tall man was a grand wizard, the head of the coven, or group, of witches Tituba had mentioned. He was the lord of hell, the angel of darkness, a life-threatening seducer and tempter. Samuel Parris wrote that "his rage is vehement and terrible." No wonder the children suffered.

Tituba confessed that she had attempted to murder children while she was in the form of a specter. (A specter is a ghostly image—a visible, disembodied spirit that haunts or perturbs the mind.) The other witches and the devil had pulled and hauled and made her go with them to Dr. Griggs's house, she said. They told her to kill Elizabeth Hubbard with a knife. Later, at Thomas Putnam's house, the witches tried to slit the throat of 12-year-old Ann Putnam Jr.—again with a knife (the weapon Medea had used).

Tituba probably had never heard of Medea, but the magistrates and ministers undoubtedly had. Schooled in an age when the Bible and ancient literature—including Greek and Roman mythology—were central to all learning, they surely would have encountered the story of Medea. In relation to witchcraft, Medea's deed and the biblical mandate "Thou shalt not suffer a witch to live" (Exodus 22:18) shaped the beliefs and legal practices of the era. Tituba was fortunate, however. The advice was only selectively followed in Salem Village. Those who confessed were not executed. The magistrates reasoned that witches who confessed had repented of their sins, and the devil was no longer with them. Besides, they were useful as witnesses against those who insisted they were innocent. Those who defended their innocence in spite of the testimony of confessed witches and spectral evidence of the afflicted were hanged.

Tituba's confession affected the outcome of the witch trials in an important way. Her confession gave credibility to the girls' claims of seeing specters, which made it possible for them to identify witches. Once spectral sight—the ability to see specters—was established as

Many people confessed to practicing witchcraft during the 1692 trials. Those who confessed were not executed.

an actual phenomenon, as fact, the girls' accusations became believable. At the time, people believed that a possessed person was clairvoyant—that he or she had a foreknowledge of events. The supposedly "possessed" girls could hear and see things other people couldn't. Because people believed in this phenomenon, the girls' testimonies and accusations were taken at face value, instead of as hoaxes or hallucinations. The court accepted the girls' stories as proof, and there was no defense against that sort of proof. The belief in evidence that included specters was strong and widespread.

The three accused women—Tituba Indian, Sarah Good, and Sarah Osborne—went to the Boston jail to await trial, but the magistrates remained in Salem Village to question the afflicted. The other witches and their wizard had yet to be named.

Within a week, Ann Putnam Jr. cried out Martha Corey's name, but Ann's parents made her hush. Corey, after all, was an upstanding member of the Reverend Parris's congregation. She did, however, oppose the witchcraft proceedings. Corey referred to the afflicted girls as "distracted people" and refused to believe they were bewitched.

Two weeks later, Abigail Williams interrupted a sermon, crying, "Look where Goodwife Corey sits upon the beam suckling her yellow bird betwixt her fingers!" Ann Putnam Jr. instantly said she saw the same image, but Martha Corey, who was in church that Sunday, only smiled. She had been told that Mercy Lewis and Ann Putnam Jr. had accused her earlier, but her reputation as a good, hardworking Christian woman who attended church every Sabbath had shielded her from their cries. Suddenly, that shield failed. She was arrested the day after Abigail pointed at her specter.

Martha Corey's examination was the last one Betty Parris attended. Her mother apparently did not want her daughter to participate in anymore witch-hunting. Betty was entrusted to an uncle and aunt, her mother's relations. Betty continued to suffer fits while at her aunt and uncle's house. According to the Reverend Lawson, "Captain Stephen Sewall [Betty's uncle] informed me Betty Parris had sore fits at his house . . . [and] she related that the great Man in Black came to her, and told her if she would be ruled by him, she should have whatsoever she desired. . . . Mrs. Sewall [then] told the child, it was the Divel, and he was a Lyar . . . and [she] bid her tell him so if he came again: which she did." Soon Betty stopped suffering fits.

Meanwhile, Gertrude Pope, a middle-aged woman known as a gossip, had begun to suffer fits. She was at Martha Corey's interrogation, together with the other afflicted people. Magistrate Corwin and the Reverend Lawson recorded the evidence of Martha Corey's extraordinary witch powers. Whenever she bit her lip, the young women's teeth clamped down on their lips and they cried out in pain; whenever Martha folded her hands in front of her, the girls screamed that she pinched them, and the backs of their hands were visibly bruised. When Martha leaned against the chair in front of her, Gertrude Pope doubled over, complaining that witch Corey was tearing her bowels out.

Martha Corey showed great insensitivity toward these afflictions. She even laughed at Gertrude Pope's complaint, whereupon Pope threw first her muff and then a shoe at Corey, the shoe striking Martha on the head.

Martha Corey soon joined Tituba and the others in the Boston prison. Her indictment marked a frightening change of course. She was the first "gospel woman" in the history of New England to be arrested and imprisoned on the charge of witchcraft. Previous cases had all involved women of questionable reputation or low status, women like Tituba, Osborne, and Good.

Another change occurred when John Proctor intervened in the accusations. Proctor was a prosperous farmer and investor, a man in good standing with his neighbors and church. He had boasted to Samuel Sibley that he had cured his family's maidservant, Mary Warren. Sibley later testified in curt that Proctor told him, "When she was first taken with fits, he kept her close to the [spinning]wheel and threatened to thrash her, and then she had no more fits." It was not an empty boast. Mary Warren herself said that she and her friends were merely distracted when in their fits, as with a temporary madness. The magistrates, she said, should pay no attention to what they said during their fits, because the girls themselves did not know what they said.

Soon an arrest warrant went out for Mary Warren. Abigail Williams said she had seen Mary sign the devil's book, and Mary—in spectral form—pinched her and hurt her. Abigail and the others also accused John Proctor's wife, Elizabeth. When Proctor came to his wife's defense, they accused and arrested him as well. Later, authorities also arrested three of his children. While he sat in prison, Proctor's cattle, furniture, and other goods were confiscated, sold, or destroyed. His prosperous farm became a wasteland. His remaining children were left destitute and had to move in with relatives.

This pattern of accusing and arresting several members of a family continued. The matronly Rebecca Nurse and her sisters, Mary Esty and Sarah Cloyce, were arrested—even though all three were well-educated, devout Christians. A robust five-year-old, Dorcas Good, openly confessed that she was a witch—probably because she wanted to be with her imprisoned mother, Sarah Good. Dorcas saw her shackled mother give birth in April. A few weeks later, the infant died. The sickly Sarah Osborne also died in prison.

By the end of May 1692, the prisons were full. Close to 100 people had been arrested on the charge of witchcraft, and bail (temporary release of a prisoner) had been denied. As yet, no one had been tried by a jury. The magistrates were waiting for a new charter and the appointment of a new governor. In 1684 the English king, James II, had revoked the old 1628 charter, so the colony was operating without an official government. For the citizens of Massachusetts Bay Colony, that meant even the titles to their homes and farms were uncertain. The situation made people uneasy. Some people looked for a scapegoat—someone or some group to blame for their problems. Others saw an opportunity to expand their landholdings since there were no laws to prevent them from doing so.

Sir William Phips and the Reverend Increase Mather had sailed to London in 1688 to plead with their majesties William and Mary, the new king and queen of England. Phips wanted weapons and provisions to help fight the French and the Indians. Increase Mather, the president of Harvard College and the father of Cotton Mather, wanted their majesties to accept the new charter he had helped draft. When

Phips's ship finally sailed into Boston Harbor, there was great celebration. He announced that the new charter had been accepted and
he had been appointed governor.

Upon his return, Governor Phips's first concern was with the
French and Indian wars. He called together a militia and prepared to
go north. When he learned that the prisons were full of people accused of witchcraft, Phips appointed Lieutenant Governor William
Stoughton to act as chief justice. Phips granted Stoughton permission
to open court and try the witchcraft cases.

Justice Stoughton opened the Court of Oyer and Terminer (a Latin
term that means "to hear and determine") in the town of Salem, on
June 2, 1692. The presiding judges "were persons of the best prudence
and figure that could then be pitched upon," Phips later wrote. The
accused thought they would finally find justice, since the best minds
in Massachusetts were sitting in judgment. Surely the girls' outcries
would be dismissed.

*William Stoughton, chief
justice of the Court of Oyer
and Terminer*

Bridget Bishop was the first to be tried. She had been accused of witchcraft in April. Bishop, a woman in her late fifties, wore a lace-trimmed scarlet bodice. She was twice widowed and married to a third husband. It was rumored that she had been unfaithful to all three husbands. She was a shrewd businesswoman who ran a prosperous inn. During questioning, Bishop said she did not know what a witch was, but then she said, "If I were such a person, you would know it." The justices took this statement as an admission of guilt and a veiled threat. Bishop insisted she was innocent, although she admitted that she had long been thought a witch.

John and William Bly, two laborers who testified against her, said that Bridget had hired them to take down the cellar walls of her old house. In the course of their labor, they found—stuck between the rocks—several knotted rag dolls. The dolls had been stuck repeatedly with headless pins. Their testimony seemed to prove that Bridget practiced black magic. The justices found her guilty on June 2. On

The wash drawing on the left illustrates the hanging of Bridget Bishop, who was convicted of witchcraft. Her death warrant is on the right.

June 8, William Stoughton signed her death warrant. On June 10, George Corwin, High Sheriff of Essex County, escorted Bridget Bishop to the gallows, where she was hanged.

Cotton Mather later noted about the case that "there was little occasion to prove the witchcraft, it being Evident and Notorious to all Beholders." Bridget's speedy trial and execution sent shudders through the rest of the accused. Evidently the justices were no more inclined to believe them than the magistrates who had originally questioned the accused. Admissible evidence at the Court of Oyer and Terminer included

◆ self-incriminating testimony (testimony against oneself)

◆ the inability of the accused to say the Lord's Prayer without error

◆ the accusations of those who confessed guilt (as when Tituba had named Good and Osborne)

◆ the spectral and nonspectral testimony of outside witnesses (spectral testimony against Bridget Bishop, for example, included statements from men who said her specter had visited them at night in their beds)

◆ the spectral testimony of the afflicted

◆ the discovery of the devil's mark on the body of the accused (The accused was taken into a small room, stripped naked, and closely examined by people of the same sex. The mark of the devil was said to look like a small red circle and was generally found somewhere near the genitals.)

◆ the pin test (When a devil's mark was found, it was pierced with a pin. If the mark did not bleed or hurt, people believed the devil had magically caused it.)

◆ the touch test, in which the accused was asked—and sometimes forced—to touch the afflicted when in their fits. This test was based on the belief that the tormenting specter must, upon contact, return to its owner. Thus, if a fit stopped when the accused person touched the afflicted person, that proved the specter of the accused had indeed been the cause of the affliction.

The use of the touch test, the amount and type of evidence coming from the afflicted, and even their presence at court caused more

This 1853 oil painting by T. H. Matteson is titled Examination of a Witch. *The women examining the body of the accused are looking for a small red circle. If the mark did not bleed or hurt when pricked with a pin, people believed the devil had magically caused it.*

than a dozen Boston-area ministers to openly question court proceedings. A few judges also questioned the wisdom of permitting the afflicted to attend court. They wanted the screeching, thrashing girls removed and found their fits unseemly and improper.

Chief Justice Stoughton disagreed with their objections. He insisted that all evidence should be taken into account, including the testimony of the afflicted girls, and that the afflicted must be present so the judges could see the immediate effects of witchcraft. Judge Nathaniel Saltonstall resigned his seat in protest. The afflicted girls soon accused him of witchcraft, but his friend Judge Samuel Sewall told the girls they were mistaken. Saltonstall was never arrested. Magistrate Jonathan Corwin was appointed in Saltonstall's place, and court reconvened on June 28.

Meanwhile, Cotton Mather had assured some other Boston ministers that none of the prisoners would be convicted on spectral evidence alone. He drafted a statement supporting the Court of Oyer and Terminer and got 12 Boston ministers to sign it, including his own father, Increase Mather, and Samuel Willard of Old South Church. When both of these men withdrew their support about a month later, they too were accused of witchcraft.

Sarah Good was the second person to be tried. She stood accused, among other things, of murdering the infant she had given birth to in prison. She was found guilty and was condemned to die. Also tried and condemned were Susannah Martin, Elizabeth How, Sarah Wilds, and Rebecca Nurse.

Friends of Rebecca Nurse presented the court with a petition signed by 39 people, including Ann Putnam's uncle and aunt, in defense of Rebecca's good character. Eleven people stood witness in her favor. Testimony against her was weak and mostly spectral. The jury found her not guilty.

Immediately following pronouncement of this verdict, the afflicted girls tumbled to the floor in horrible shrieking fits, wailing that Rebecca's specter was killing them. On seeing this, Justice Stoughton asked the jury if they had considered the words of the defendant, spoken when Elizabeth Hobbs and her daughter had been brought in to

The trial of Rebecca Nurse, as depicted at the Salem Witch Museum in Salem, Massachusetts

testify. Court records showed that on seeing these two confessed witches, Rebecca Nurse had said, "What, do these give in Evidence against me now? They used to come among us." Was this not an admission of Rebecca having been among the witches of the coven? the judge asked.

Juror Thomas Fisk turned to Rebecca Nurse and asked what she had meant by the words, "They used to come among us," but Rebecca did not answer. The jury went out a second time and found her guilty.

Later, Rebecca Nurse sent an explanation to the court. She said that she was hard-of-hearing and had been overcome with sorrow. She had not heard the juror's question. As to her remark, "They used to come among us," she had only meant that Elizabeth Hobbs and her daughter used to be in the same prison cell with her and some others. But the explanation arrived too late. The court had already condemned her to death.

Rebecca's friends petitioned Governor Phips for a reprieve of her sentence. He granted their request, and Rebecca was temporarily safe. When the afflicted girls heard about the reprieve, they cried out against her. Several Salem men asked the governor to rescind (take back) his reprieve, which he did.

Rebecca Nurse, Sarah Good, Sarah Wilds, Elizabeth How, and Susannah Martin were hanged on July 19. Little Dorcas Good spent three additional months in prison. Her father, a poor laborer, finally collected enough money to bail her out in early October.

The morning after the executions, Rebecca Nurse's body was missing. Her family had come at night, taken her down from the gallows, and held a secret Christian burial service—secret because it was against the law to give a Christian burial to a condemned person. Authorities dumped the other four bodies in a shallow grave behind the gallows. The place became known as "Gallows Hill."

Meanwhile, Ann Putnam Jr. and Mary Walcott were invited to Andover, a town northwest of Salem Village. Goodwife Ballard was dying, and the doctors could not find the cause. Joseph Ballard and the assistant pastor of his church, the Reverend Thomas Barnard, thought it might be witchcraft. The two girls confirmed the men's suspicions. They saw a specter at the head of the bed and one sitting on the woman's stomach. The Reverend Barnard decided to repeat the experiment. He took the girls to another sickbed in another home, and then to yet another, and another. The girls saw specters in every case, but could name no witches because they didn't know the people in Andover. To solve the problem, the Reverend Barnard invited the women of Andover to submit to the touch test. Sure of their innocence, the women agreed.

The results of the touch test were overwhelming. Sixty-seven women were arrested. Desperate family members and threatening ministers badgered the accused women for hours. They wanted the women to confess—and thus avoid being hanged. No one who had confessed had been hanged, a fact that never changed.

Many Andover women finally did break down and confess. While in prison, however, they heartily repented for having "belied" themselves. They sent letters and petitions to the governor, male family members, and Boston ministers they hoped would be sympathetic to their cause. Among the ministers they wrote to was Increase Mather. He began visiting them in prison and recording their complaints and fears.

Martha Carrier became the first Andover resident to stand trial. She had been arrested in May, while visiting family members in Salem Village. All four of her children were imprisoned as well. Her two eldest sons, aged 15 and 17, flatly denied that their mother was a witch. To get them to confess, jailers tied the boys' neck and heels, a form of torture that caused nosebleeds. The torture worked. Both boys confessed that their mother was a witch and that they themselves had been witches for one month. The boys' younger brother and sister, aged 10 and 7, probably saw their brothers being tortured and undoubtedly heard them scream. The younger children confessed as quickly and easily as Dorcas Good had, but in the end, their testimony and that of their older brothers was not allowed in court. John Proctor had written a letter of complaint to Increase Mather and Samuel Willard, revealing the court's unlawful use of force and threats. Proctor's own son had been tied neck and heels. Proctor also

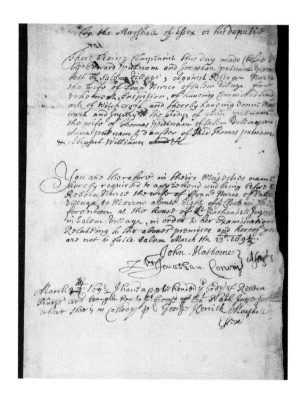

The arrest warrant for Rebecca Nurse, who was accused of witchcraft

accused the court of relying almost entirely on spectral evidence in convicting himself, his wife, John Willard, George Jacobs Sr., and Martha Carrier.

Proctor's letter prompted Increase Mather to attend the trial of the Reverend George Burroughs, then in progress. Mather wanted to see if Proctor was right about the court's use of spectral evidence. Burroughs, the only minister to be arrested, was not asked to recite the Lord's Prayer. Nor was he permitted to speak in his own defense. Burroughs had been widowed twice and had then married a third time. He had not been popular with his congregation when he was the minister at the church in Salem Village, the same one the Reverend Parris now served. He was equally disliked by former in-laws, who believed he had beaten his first two wives to death. They testified against him, as did many others. George Burroughs was short, yet exceptionally strong and fleet-footed. He had shown off his strength at taverns on many occasions. According to witnesses, such unnatural strength had to come from the devil.

During cross-examination, Burroughs gave feeble replies, as if suffering memory lapses—or worse—as if caught lying. Though spectral evidence was heard, other evidence weighed heavily against him. Increase Mather went away convinced that George Burroughs had been fairly tried and condemned.

John Proctor, Martha Carrier, George Burroughs, George Jacob Sr., and John Willard were hanged on August 19. Elizabeth Proctor was granted a reprieve because she was three months pregnant.

From the steps of the gallows ladder, the Reverend Burroughs was finally permitted to preach a sermon defending his innocence. He urged the judges of Oyer and Terminer Court to reexamine the methods they were using. While he spoke, the afflicted children pointed at the ladder and said they saw the devil dictating to Burroughs. Undaunted, Burroughs closed with the Lord's Prayer, recited flawlessly

Increase Mather was the president of Harvard College, the oldest institution of higher learning in the United States. Cotton Mather was his son.

using Satan's power to perform miracles? "It were better," he said, "that 10 suspected Witches should escape than that one innocent Person should be condemned."

Governor Phips, who had returned from the war front, followed Increase Mather's advice. On October 12, Phips wrote to the privy council in London that he now "found that the Devill had taken upon him the name and shape of severall people who were doubtless innocent." Even the governor's wife had been accused. On October 29, 1692, Governor Phips dissolved the Court of Oyer and Terminer.

On November 25, the general court of the colony created a superior court to try the remaining prisoners. No spectral evidence was allowed. By January 1693, 49 of the 52 remaining prisoners had been

The Trial of George Jacobs, *accused of witchcraft. The painting is by T. H. Matteson.*

In this diorama—a realistically sculpted scene—Giles Corey is being pressed to death in an attempt to force him to testify in court. He refused to do so.

acquitted. The other three were pardoned. Inability to pay prison fees left a few behind bars until April. Among them was Tituba. The Reverend Samuel Parris refused to pay her prison fees, so the jailer sold her to another master.

At first, ministers thought that praying and fasting might cure the afflicted girls.

THREE

DIVINE PUNISHMENT

"There is more to be said than hath been for the clearing up of difficulties about the matter of witchcraft."

—The Reverend John Higginson

THE REVEREND DEODAT LAWSON WROTE THE FIRST history of Salem witchcraft. His *A Brief and True Narrative of Some Remarkable Passages Relating to People Afflicted by Witchcraft at Salem Village*, published in April 1692, provides an eyewitness account of events that took place in March and early April.

Lawson's narrative begins with his arrival at Ingersoll Inn, where he met and talked with Mary Walcott. Later, Walcott suddenly cried out in pain and complained that her wrist hurt. Lawson and some others examined her wrist by candlelight and found teeth marks.

The next day, while visiting the Reverend Samuel Parris in his home, Lawson saw Abigail Williams run recklessly back and forth, her arms stretched out as if she would fly. "Whish! Whish! Whish!" she cried, then stopping short, said, "There is Goodwife Nurse. Do you not see her? Why, there she stands!" But Lawson saw only an empty space. He marveled when Abigail shouted, "I won't! I won't! I won't take it!" as if Rebecca Nurse actually stood there. "I do not know what book it is," she continued. "I am sure it is none of God's book. It is the devil's book for ought I know." Suddenly, she ran into the hearth, threw coals about the room, and tried to fly up the chimney. The Reverend Parris pulled her out.

An illustration of a witch signing the devil's black book

On the following Sabbath, Abigail Williams and Gertrude Pope blurted insulting remarks during the worship service. "Stand up and name your text," ordered Abigail. When Lawson, who had been invited to preach, read the title of his sermon, she complained, "It is a long text." He had hardly begun his sermon when Gertrude Pope interrupted, "Now there is enough of that!" That same Sunday, Martha Corey's specter was said to have appeared in the rafters, although she was sitting on a bench.

Lawson gave an account of Martha Corey's interrogation and then described Ann Putnam Sr. lying in bed, gasping as if she were being choked, her limbs extended and stiff. Suddenly, she sat up and began talking to Rebecca Nurse, though her eyes were shut. Lawson again could not see Rebecca, yet Ann carried on a long conversation with her, scolding her for pretending to be a good Christian when she was a witch and a friend of the devil.

Lawson closed his narrative with a list of observations he had made about the afflicted and the accused. When in their fits, he wrote, "They are tempted to be witches, are shewed the list of the names of others, and are tortured, because they will not yield." Also during their fits, "When the accused person was present, the afflicted people saw her likeness in other places." Additionally, when in their fits, their limbs would twist and stiffen in postures that "no well person could screw his body into, and as to the violence also it is preternatural, being much beyond the ordinary force of the same person when they are in their right mind." During these fits, "they did in the assembly mutually cure each other, even with a touch of their hand." The afflicted could also foretell "when another's fit was a-coming and would say, 'Look to her! She will have a fit presently,' which fell out accordingly."

The accused, wrote Lawson, "are reported by the Afflicted People to keep dayes of Fast and dayes of Thanksgiving, and Sacraments, Satan endeavours to Transforme himself to an Angel of Light and . . . Satan Rages Principally amongst the Visible Subjects of Christ's Kingdom [churchgoers] and makes use of some of them to Afflict others, that Christ's Kingdom may be divided against itself." And so it was, with Christians accusing and condemning other Christians.

Of the accused, Lawson wrote, "In time of examination, they seemed little affected" by the sufferings of the afflicted, "though all the spectators were much grieved to see it." They were also very powerful, for by their natural movements, they produced preternatural suffering in the afflicted, "so that they are their own image, without any poppits [puppets] of wax or otherwise." Yet as soon as an accused person was in prison, his or her specter no longer tormented the afflicted. Troubling to Lawson was the fact that most of the accused were "visible subjects of Christ's Kingdom."

The Reverend Cotton Mather wrote a second history of Salem witchcraft, called *Wonders of the Invisible World.* William Stoughton had commissioned the work, which was published in October 1692.

Cotton Mather did not write an eyewitness report. Although he attended the executions, his book does not mention the final moments of the accused. It focuses on their trials, which he did not attend. To write his history, he borrowed court records and focused on five cases—those of George Burroughs, Bridget Bishop, Susannah Martin,

Although he did not attend the trials, Cotton Mather wrote a book about them. His book The Wonders of the Invisible World *is based on court records.*

Elizabeth How, and Martha Carrier. "I report matters not as an advocate but as a historian," he stated in his introduction. He then proceeded to write with the flowery, passionate language of a man defending a cause. He treated the testimony of the afflicted with sympathy and the testimony of repentant, confessed "witches" as completely believable. Mather emphasized nonspectral evidence given by outside witnesses and the self-condemning words of the accused. The court, he argued, did not pass sentence on spectral evidence alone.

Mather went on to assert that the outbreak of witchcraft fulfilled a prophecy made by a witch who had been executed years ago. The devil, she had warned, was plotting against the parishioners, sowing seeds of division so the church in New England would fall. Knowing that the church was sharply divided over the possibility of killing innocent victims, Cotton Mather attempted reconciliation. "If a drop of innocent blood should be shed in the prosecution of witchcrafts among us, how unhappy are we!" he wrote. But in the same paragraph he wrote, "On the other side, if the storm of justice do now fall only on the heads of those guilty witches and wretches which have defiled our land, how happy!" He finished with a number of "curiosities" intended to prove that only the guilty had been executed.

About five years later, a sense of guilt spread among many of the judges, ministers, and jurors who had been involved in the Court of Oyer and Terminer. When crops failed, loved ones died, the land became impoverished, and the prolonged war continued, some people began to fear that God was punishing them. The council and governor

In this diorama, Ann Putnam is repenting for her behavior during the Salem trials.

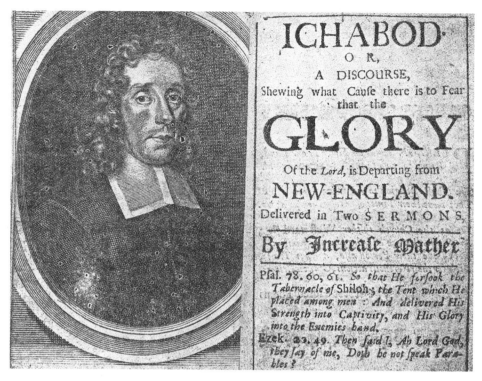

Increase Mather published two sermons "showing what cause there is to fear that the GLORY of the Lord, is departing from New England."

published declarations urging people to pray and ask God's forgiveness for past sins, especially "the errors of his servants in the late tragedy" at Salem. Judge Samuel Sewall, the Reverend Samuel Parris, the Reverend John Hale, juror Thomas Fisk and the other 11 jury members, and even the formerly afflicted Ann Putnam Jr. issued statements of repentance and read them in front of the congregations in their various churches.

In 1697 the Reverend John Hale went a step further. He wrote a history in which he stated that the court erred because of ignorance. Innocent people had died with the guilty. For the sake of their surviving relations, he encouraged the government to make amends and clear the good names of innocent people who had been condemned.

He warned that God would continue to punish Massachusetts if
amends were not made. "I would humbly propose whether it be not
expedient, that some what more should be publickly done than yet
hath, for clearing the good name and reputation of some that have
suffered upon this account, against whom the evidence of their guilt
was slender, and the grounds for charity for them more convinc-
ing. . . . None of their surviving relations [should] suffer reproach
upon that account."

Hale had been troubled by the executions of 1692 for a long time.
"I have had a deep sence of the sad consequence of mistakes in matters Capital; and their impossibility of recovering when compleated,"
he wrote. The men of 1692 meant well and sought God's guidance
and direction. "But," he continued, "such was the darkness of that
day, the tortures and lamentations of the afflicted, and the power of
former presidents, that we walked in the clouds, and could not see
our way."

Since then, the colony had learned from its mistakes. The evidence
used to prove witchcraft was "too slender to evidence the crime they
were brought to prove," Hale concluded. Such evidence would no
longer be accepted in any court. Hale's *A Modest Enquiry into the
Nature of Witchcraft* was completed in 1697, but it was not published
until 1702, apparently because printers were afraid to publish so bold
a thesis.

MORE
WONDERS
OF THE
INVISIBLE WORLD:

Or, The Wonders of the

𝔍𝔫𝔳𝔦𝔰𝔦𝔟𝔩𝔢 𝔚𝔬𝔯𝔩𝔡,

Display'd in Five Parts.

Part I. An Account of the Sufferings of *Margaret Rule*, Written by the Reverend Mr. C. *Mather*.

P. II. Several Letters to the Author, &c. And his Reply relating to Witchcraft.

P. III. The Differences between the Inhabitants of *Salem*-Village, and Mr. *Parris* their Minister, in *New-England*.

P. IV. Letters of a Gentleman uninterested, Endeavouring to prove the received Opinions about Witchcraft to be Orthodox. With short Essays to their Answers.

P. V. A short Historical Accout of Matters of Fact in that Affair.

To which is added, A Postscript relating to a Book intitled, *The Life of Sir* WILLIAM PHIPS.

Collected by *Robert Calef*, Merchant, of *Boston* in *New-England*.

Licensed and Entred according to Order.

LONDON:
Printed for *Nath. Hillar*, at the *Princes-Arms*, in *Leaden-Hall-street*, over against St. *Mary-Ax*, and *Joseph Collyer*, at the *Golden-Bible*, on *London-Bridge*. 1700.

---— ❧ FOUR ❧ ———

RATIONALISM VS. WITCHCRAFT

"Truth shall and will be truth in spite of men and devils."
—Robert Calef, *More Wonders of the Invisible World*

EIGHT YEARS AFTER COTTON MATHER'S *WONDERS of the Invisible World* was published, Robert Calef published *More Wonders of the Invisible World.* He could not find a printer in New England willing to publish it because they thought it was a libel against Cotton Mather. So Calef sent his manuscript to London for publication. The British publisher then shipped copies back to New England, where they were sold.

Robert Calef was a prosperous cloth merchant from Boston and a friend of Thomas Brattle. Brattle, a distinguished mathematician and astronomer who had traveled among learned circles in Europe, had probably met John Locke (1634–1704). Brattle and Calef had undoubtedly read Locke's famous book *An Essay Concerning Human Understanding,* published in 1690.

Locke was influenced by a philosophy called rationalism, which evolved in the 1600s out of the works of philosopher-mathematicians René Descartes (1596–1650) and Baruch (also called Benedict) Spinoza (1632–1677). Locke took their complex rationalist thinking and offered it to the average English reader—men like Robert Calef—in a format that was easy to understand. English merchants were among

Cotton Mather, left, was sharply criticized by later historians who wrote about the Salem trials.

Locke's first converts to rationalist thinking.

The rationalists were tired of intellectual arguments based entirely on the writings of ancient and medieval philosophers like Aristotle (384–322 B.C.) and Thomas Aquinas (A.D. 1224–1274). The rationalists did not even want to limit their understanding of life to Biblical interpretation or to the value of conventions and dangers of popular superstitions. Instead, they based their conclusions on observable, measurable, actual experiences and on reason.

Robert Calef's book had a volcanic impact. His rationalistic approach to the subject permanently altered the way historians wrote about witchcraft at Salem. Historians in the eighteenth and nineteenth centuries viewed Calef as a courageous, reasonable, and capable opponent of the witchcraft delusion. Many of the same historians condemned Cotton Mather as a self-deluded, self-righteous, overly ambitious minister and politician—the very label Calef stamped on him.

Calef's book is arranged in five parts. Parts one and two focus on Cotton Mather's published studies and methods for treating the affliction of witchcraft. Calef mocks Mather's treatments as a study in child's games and gullibility. Part three of Calef's book consists of a collection of petitions and letters written by people at Salem Village. Complaints written by members of the Nurse family, and signed by many others, demanded a public apology from the Reverend Samuel Parris for his role in the witchcraft trials. In November 1694, Parris finally submitted a statement of repentance. He confessed to having erred out of ignorance. He wrote, "I question not but God sometimes suffers the Devil (as of late) to afflict in the shape of not only innocent but pious people, or so delude the senses of the afflicted that from such people . . . I do heartily, fervently, and humbly beseech pardon . . . of all my mistakes and trespasses in so weighty a matter."

Part four of Calef's book is an exchange of letters between himself and a Scottish ship's chaplain. The chaplain defends the prosecution of witches as a necessary Christian duty. Calef denounces all efforts

In his book, More Wonders of the Invisible World, *Robert Calef condemns witch-hunts as being un-Christian and based on superstition.*

to discover and execute witches as inherently superstitious and un-Christian. In part five, Calef presents a string of examples illustrating how shabby witchcraft evidence is and what it can cost in terms of lost life, honor, property, and peace.

The subtitle of part five is "A Short Historical Account of Matters of Fact . . . Touching the Supposed Witchcraft in New England." Calef's history begins with a rewrite of Deodat Lawson's narrative. Calef then goes on to describe how, at the interrogation of Elizabeth Proctor, her husband, John, came to her defense by denouncing the afflicted as frauds. Immediately following his statement of defense, he himself was accused of witchcraft.

Calef relates Captain Nathaniel Cary's account of his wife's ordeal. Cary wrote, "I was only as a Spectator, my Wife also was there part of the time, but no notice taken of her by the afflicted, except once or twice they came to her and asked her name." He had come because he had heard his wife had been accused of witchcraft by one of the afflicted girls. Cary asked Reverend Hale if he might have a word in private with the girl who had accused his wife. Cary was told he

An illustration of victims found guilty of practicing witchcraft on their way to the gallows, as it appeared in the Boston Herald *on May 14, 1930*

Excerpts from Calef's Closing Argument

Robert Calef believed accusing innocent people, such as Rebecca Nurse, of witchcraft was a dishonor to God.

"As long as men suffer themselves to be Poison'd in their Education, and be grounded in a False Belief by the Books of the Heathen; As long as the Devil shall be believed to have Natural Power, to Act above and against a course of Nature; As long as the Witches shall be believed to have a Power to Commission him; As long as Devils' Testimony, by the pretended afflicted, shall be received as more valid to Condemn than Pleas of Not Guilty to acquit; As long as the Accused shall have their Lives and Liberties confirmed and restored to them, upon their Confessing themselves Guilty; As long as the Accused shall be forc't to undergo Hardships and Torments for their not Confessing; As long as Tets for the Devil to Suck are searched for upon the Bodies of the accused, as a token of guilt; As long as the Lord's Prayer shall be profaned, by being made a Test, who are culpable; As long as Witchcraft, Sorcery, Familiar Spirits, and Necromancy shall be [used] to discover who [is a] Witch; So long [as the] Innocent suffer as Witches, God will be Daily dishonoured, and his Judgements can be expected to continue."

could meet with her that evening at Ingersoll Inn, but when he and his wife retired to the inn, they found all the afflicted there with the magistrates. "Now instead of one accuser, they all came in, who began to tumble down like Swine. . . . In a short time they cried out, 'Cary.'" His wife was immediately arrested and questioned. Among the afflicted was John Indian. "He now (when before the Justices) fell down and tumbled about like a Hog, but said nothing. The Justices asked the Girls, who afflicted the Indian? They answered she (meaning my wife); the Justices ordered her to touch him, in order to cure him, but her head must be turned another way, least instead of curing, she should make him worse . . . her hand being guided to take hold of his; but Indian took hold . . . and pulled her down on the Floor, in a barbarous manner." In the end, she was imprisoned, but Nathaniel Cary was able to rescue her. Together, they fled to New York for sanctuary.

Following Cary's account is one by Captain John Alden. He also escaped from prison. Alden called the afflicted "wenches who played their juggling tricks, falling down, crying out, and staring into people's faces." At first, the afflicted accused a lieutenant standing next to Alden, but the magistrates told them they were mistaken. Then a man standing behind one of the afflicted bent over and whispered in her ear. "Alden! Alden!" she cried out. He was arrested that same day.

Calef, in full agreement with Alden's view of the afflicted, describes an event that took place during Sarah Good's trial. One of the afflicted shrieked that she had been stabbed by Sarah's specter. The girl produced a knife shard that she said had been embedded in her chest. A young man from the audience then stepped forward and told the court that he had broken a knife the day before and had seen this same afflicted person pick up a sliver from his blade. He produced the rest of the knife. The shard fit exactly, yet the girl was only lightly reprimanded and allowed to go on accusing people.

Calef used the fate of the Jacobs family as an example of justice gone so far awry as to be cruel. The court condemned George Jacobs Sr. to death on spectral evidence alone. The confession of his granddaughter, Margaret Jacobs, was used against him. In a letter to her fa-

The former home of George Jacobs, who was executed for allegedly practicing witchcraft

ther, Margaret retracted her confession, saying she was not a witch, but being afraid for her life had said that she was. Now she heartily repented, seeing that her grandfather was hanged and her poor distracted mother arrested. She blamed herself for these events.

When Margaret's mother was arrested, her small children were left standing in the yard, crying. They would have died of hunger and cold if a kindly neighbor had not taken them in. Meanwhile, Grandmother Jacobs, who had no money and nothing else to give toward payment of prison fees, was stripped of her wedding ring by a sheriff who came to collect.

Calef also highlights the retrial of Rebecca Nurse and a petition written by Mary Esty. Mary did not ask that her life be spared if it pleased God to take it from her. Instead, she begged the judges to reexamine the methods they were using. "That no more Innocent blood be shed I would humbly begg of you that your honors would be plesed to examine theis Afflicted People strictly and keepe them apart some time and Likewise to try some of these confesing wichis, I being confident there is severall of them has belyed themselves."

Calef next examines Cotton Mather's history of the trials. He quotes select phrases, like "rampant hag," which Mather used to describe Martha Carrier. Calef pointedly accuses Mather of writing "more like an advocate than an historian."

Calef's closing argument is equally sharp. He writes:

> "He is in a false belief, about the power of Witches and Devils (who thinks he is) driving away Devils by brushing and striking with a sword or stick." As long as men swat with their hands and swing with their swords at empty air believing that by so doing, they inflict wounds on the specter of a person far away; as long as flea bites are called devil's tits; as long as the Lord's Prayer is used as a test to magically discover the profane; as long as the testimony of possessed children is treated as fact; as long as confessed witches are spared and innocent people are hanged; as long as necromancy is used as evidence in a court of law (as it was when the afflicted said they saw the ghosts of George Burroughs's dead wives, and the ghosts told the girls that Burroughs had murdered them); as long as the government refused to clear the names of the innocent and recompense families whom unscrupulous sheriffs impoverished; as long as ministers argue that there is such a thing as witchcraft, the rage of the righteous God will consume New England.

In 1710 the government cleared the names of all but five of those who had been executed. During the next 40 to 50 years, families of the accused filed complaints and received compensation. But many people still clung to old superstitions. Some people thought they saw the ghosts of pirates. Others believed houses and woods were haunted. A few widows began reading palms, holding seances, and making prophecies—without fear of being imprisoned or hanged as witches. Witchcraft was no longer considered a crime that could be prosecuted.

In *The History of the Colony and Province of Massachusetts*, written in 1750, Thomas Hutchinson refers to the Salem witchcraft trials as a "delusion," and he calls Calef's book "an indictment of the seventeenth century." Calef's book was reprinted in 1796, 1823, 1828,

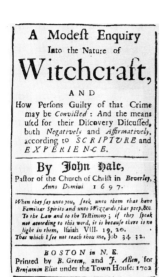

John Hale wrote A Modest Enquiry into the Nature of Witchcraft *in 1697.*

1861, an 1866. Prior to the 1866 reprint, historian W. Elliot Woodward printed the Salem witchcraft court records. The original handwritten records had become torn, damaged, and difficult to read. Woodward's edition made it easier for historians to research the trials.

In 1867 Charles W. Upham published the first comprehensive history of the Salem trials. His book, *Salem Witchcraft, with an Account of Salem Village and a History of the Opinions on Witchcraft and Kindred Subjects,* became a research reference for virtually all future histories on the subject. Upham calls the Salem trials "the witchcraft delusion of 1692." He views Calef as a reliable reporter of facts and events and Cotton Mathers as a sadly deluded man whose views of the devil contributed to his "loose interpretation of events." Rationalism prevailed among witchcraft historians for almost two centuries.

The Reverend John Hale presented a sympathetic view of the afflicted girls when he published his *Modest Inquiry* in 1702, but Robert Calef, Thomas Hutchinson, and Charles Upham viewed the afflicted as pretenders. Their rationalist assessment has generally been abandoned by most twentieth-century historians, who have explored the subject from many different points of view.

The cover photo on Radical Spirits: Spiritualism and Women's Rights in Nineteenth-Century America, *a book by Ann Braude*

———— ⊰ FIVE ⊱ ————

DIAGNOSING WITCHCRAFT

"The cause of these hysterical symptoms, of course, was not witchcraft itself but the victim's fear of it."
—Chadwick Hansen, *Witchcraft at Salem*

N THE LATE 1800S, A SURGE OF POPULAR AND scientific interest in the *occult* developed. The term occult refers to matters thought to involve supernatural or supernormal powers or some secret knowledge of them. This new interest in the occult caused historians in New England to look again at what happened in Salem Village in 1692. Psychologists and practitioners of the occult both used hypnosis—a temporary condition of altered attention in an individual.

A hypnotist uses various methods to induce (guide) hypnosis in another person. As the person responds to the methods, his or her state of attention changes. For example, the person may experience different levels of awareness, consciousness, imagination, memory, and reasoning. A hypnotized person might also become more responsive to suggestions. The word suggestion is used here to mean that which causes a physical, mental, or emotional response to a word or image by association. For example, the word red suggests a color to some people, heat to others, embarrassment to others, and blood to still others. Was it possible, historians began to wonder, that suggestions of this sort caused the afflicted people at Salem to act the way they did? Had they been hypnotized?

To Wendell Barrett and other witchcraft historians of the 1880s and 1890s, hypnotism seemed a likely explanation for the witchcraft hysteria of 1692. These historians based their theory in part on what they had observed among the occultists of their day. Until the late 1800s, most scientists considered hypnotism an occult practice. Although some scientists reject all occult practices, others believe in certain occult powers, which they call *paranormal* (outside normal awareness).

One occult practice, *spiritualism*, is the belief that spirits of the dead can communicate with the living. In the United States, the spiritualist movement began in the mid-1800s. To communicate with departed spirits, spiritualists usually meet in small gatherings called séances. An individual called a *medium* leads the séance. Spiritualists believe the medium has a special knowledge or power that ordinary people do not have. Most of the mediums at the end of the nineteenth century were female.

During a séance, a medium becomes self-hypnotized. Once she is hypnotized, she usually speaks in a voice that is different from her own, and her personality changes. Through a medium, spiritualists believe they can talk to the spirits of the dead. Mediums often claim to see the specter of a participant's departed friend or relative. The medium relates what the specter supposedly said. The medium's eyes usually remain closed throughout the séance. When the spirit leaves the medium, she frequently collapses. Some mediums suffer violent fits immediately after a spirit leaves. A medium might even scream in terror while staring at an empty corner of the room, but finally she appears normal and sensible once again.

Historians of the late 1800s recognized many similarities between what they saw among spiritualists of their day and what Lawson and others had written about the afflicted girls in Salem Village. The girls had claimed to see specters. They related what these spirits had supposedly told them about the accused. Many people had observed several of the afflicted, like Ann Putnam Sr., Mercy Lewis, Betty Hubbard, and others, speaking to specters with their eyes shut tight.

A séance during the first half of the nineteenth century, as portrayed in an unidentified woodcut

Abigail Williams and Ann Putnam Jr. had displayed altered personalities, especially in the impudent way they interrupted Sunday worship service. And all of the afflicted had on many occasions collapsed into fits, screamed in terror, and stared at seemingly empty spaces.

The way nineteenth-century believers in the occult acted in the presence of a medium seemed to correspond to the behavior of the ministers, judges, and spectators who watched when the girls had their fits. By their gestures, tone of voice, and choice of words, occult believers seemed to induce the hypnotic state and to direct the medium's responses. Was it not possible that Reverend Parris, Magistrate Hathorne, Chief Justice Stoughton, and others influenced the girls in much the same way? For example, Reverend Parris relentlessly questioned Abigail Williams and Betty Parris when their behavior changed. He believed such behavior was due to witchcraft, and he wanted to know who was tormenting them.

The suggestion of witchcraft may have caused the girls to look for a witch. They had seen Tituba make a witch cake. They had also seen cranky Sarah Good come to the door, beg for food and tobacco, and tramp away muttering. They had heard negative gossip about Sarah

Psychologists and practitioners of the occult used various methods to hypnotize an individual.

Osborne, and they may have heard people call her a witch. Perhaps the girls just told Reverend Parris what he wanted to hear.

When the wife of George Jacobs Jr. was accused and arrested, the sheriff brought the distracted woman before the girls. They did not recognize her and showed no signs of affliction until after Magistrate Hathorne suggested, "Don't you know Jacobs, the old witch?" Immediately, they cried out and collapsed into fits, as if in direct response to Hathorne's words. Likewise, Captain Alden was not recognized as a wizard until someone suggested that he was.

Even the accused seemed to have inadvertently caused a hypnotic response in the girls. When, for example, Rebecca Nurse tilted her head, or when Martha Corey clasped her hands together, or when Bridget Bishop rolled her eyes, the girls imitated their gestures, as if obeying suggestive cues.

During the late 1800s, Dr. Jean-Martin Charcot, a French neurologist, performed landmark experiments involving hypnosis. Charcot used hypnotic suggestion to induce hysteria in volunteer patients. He brought the patients to class so his students could observe the symptoms of a condition that afflicted mostly women and girls.

One of Charcot's students, Pierre Janet, later made an exhaustive study of hysteria. Janet believed hysteria was caused by split or multiple personality syndrome. He cured the disease by hypnotizing the patient, getting the patient to recall the cause of each symptom, and then helping the patient overcome each cause, until all symptoms disappeared.

In 1895 Sigmund Freud—another student of Charcot's—published a thesis relating his findings that hysteria patients need not be hypnotized to be cured and not all such patients had split personalities. He developed a method called psychoanalysis, and redefined hysteria as a broad spectrum of symptoms caused by trauma or emotional shock.

Charcot and his students believed that the symptoms of hysteria were the same as those formerly attributed to witchcraft or possession by a demon. Symptoms included: sight disorders; trances; visions of ghosts, beasts, or skeletons; hearing disorders; conversation with imagined people; anorexia; temporary paralysis of limbs; convulsions;

Dr. Jean-Martin Charcot gave clinical lectures to his students. He used hypnosis in experiments to induce hysteria.

imagined injuries—sometimes accompanied by swelling and redness; the feeling of choking or having a lump in the throat; inability to speak; frantic movement; uncontrollable weeping, laughing, or screaming; unclear, spiteful, or frightened speeches; and postconvulsion calm and good health.

Research on hysteria continued into the twentieth century. Between the 1940s and the 1980s, historians began to compare psychological descriptions of hysteria to the recorded behavior of the afflicted people in Salem Village. According to court records, Mary Warren had been carried out of the courtroom when she collapsed in a paralyzing, choking fit and could not testify. Mercy Lewis, Betty Hubbard, Ann Putnam Sr., and others had also choked, and each of them sometimes said she had a lump in her throat. Abigail Williams, Mary Walcott, Ann Putnam Jr., and others had been removed from court on several occasions because the judges and jury could not bear their uncontrollable screaming fits.

At one time or another, all of the afflicted complained that specters bit, stabbed, pinched, or strangled them. As proof, they showed the court teeth marks, pin wounds, bruises, and finger marks around their throats. About 34 people claimed to be afflicted. Twenty-nine of them were female, 21 were teenagers. Psychologists had found that most hysteria patients were female, and, according to Freud, symptoms in both male and female patients usually surfaced as a result of emotional trauma experienced during youth.

What traumatic event might have begun the witch hysteria in Salem Village? Was it Abigail's coffin in the spinning egg? Was it in the witch cake Tituba made? Was it fear of witchcraft, the devil, or divine wrath? Was it a sermon the Reverend Parris preached?

Parris received much of his support from the poorer farmers of Salem Village. To them, Parris and the village church represented stability and traditional values. The poorer farmers saw the town of Salem, with its increasingly important merchants, as a threat to their way of life. Parris and his supporters helped lead the witch-hunt. Many people who opposed Parris or had links with Salem were arrested as witches.

This engraving by Edwin A. Abbey is called The Long Sermon. *Widespread fear of the devil lent zeal to the sermons of Puritan ministers like Samuel Parris.*

In looking for clues about the cause of the witch hysteria in Salem Village, historians have probed colonial beliefs, fears, and prejudices surrounding God, the devil, magic, political and economic uncertainty, attacks by Native Americans, and the beginning of the French and Indian wars. One court ruling might have particularly affected people. Salem Village was one of five farming communities surrounding the town of Salem. As these communities grew, they sought independent township status from the general court in Boston. Citizens of an independent township did not have to pay property taxes to Salem or attend church there. They could build their own church and pay taxes to their own minister and community leaders. The minister was the town's leading citizen and colonial representative in Boston. Although the townships weren't independent of the central government in Boston, they did enjoy a level of autonomy they could not get as a suburb of Salem.

The communities at Wenham, Manchester, Marblehead, and Beverly were granted the right to become independent townships, but Salem Village was not. The court would only grant Salem Villagers an exemption from the law that required them to attend church in Salem. The angry community appealed the ruling, hired a minister, and met for worship in Salem Village. They even built their own church. By 1689, when Samuel Parris arrived, the court had granted the villagers only half of what they wanted. They could have their own parish, but they could not form an independent township. The community split

The French and Indian Wars

In 1689 the first of the four French and Indian wars broke out. English colonists fought French colonists and their Indian allies. Between 1689 and 1713, settlers along the northern and western borders of Massachusetts fought off continuous French and Indian attacks. When England and France signed a peace treaty in 1713, an era of prosperity began in Massachusetts. Dozens of towns sprang up in the central and northern part of the Massachusetts Bay Colony. The wars broke out again in the 1740s, however. They finally ended in 1763 with victory for the British.

English colonists often had to defend themselves against French and Indian raids.

Rebecca Nurse's house. Prosperous farmers, such as Francis and Rebecca Nurse, could afford to pay Salem property taxes—a situation that created friction between them and some of the poorer landowners.

when the Reverend Parris began to act like the leading citizen and representative. He was, after all, only the parish minister.

Prosperous farmers, such as Francis Nurse, Rebecca's husband, could afford to pay Salem property taxes. These farmers were satisfied with Salem representation in legal cases and dissatisfied with Samuel Parris's sense of self-importance. Meanwhile, Thomas Putnam, a poorer farmer who had just lost a lawsuit regarding his father's will in Salem, supported Parris. Putnam's wife and daughter were among the afflicted who first accused Rebecca Nurse and her sisters of witchcraft, and Thomas Putnam testified against her in court.

Historians have also studied the religious beliefs and superstitions that people clung to in Salem Village and throughout the Massachusetts Bay Colony. People practiced magic—even while they went to church and said their prayers. For example, Mary Sibley shared magic recipes and cures. Young women such as Abigail Williams and Mary Walcott used magic charms and cures. And some people practiced black magic, as Bridget Bishop seems to have done by making doll images of her enemies and sticking pins in them.

Meanwhile, ministers continually preached to these same people about the dangers of practicing magic. Magic was "of the devil," the minister said. The devil deceived people who thought magic could

Some of the accused were charged with using witch pins, such as those to the left, to torment their victims. These pins were preserved among the files of the county court at Salem.

solve their problems or show them the future. By attempting cures with spells, church leaders said, people opened the door to the devil and his legions. Hadn't the devil already turned neighbor against neighbor?

Widespread fear of the devil and every evil associated with him lent zeal to the ministers and judges involved in the witchcraft prosecutions. Even those people who went to the hanging scaffold protesting their innocence expressed the belief that the devil was responsible for their plight. They said he had deluded the afflicted children, causing them to accuse God-fearing people without knowing what they did.

Puritan children were taught to fear the devil very early in life, but they were also taught to tremble before God. Almost as soon as they could speak, toddlers began to learn that no matter how virtuous a person might be, he or she could never be sure of reaching heaven. According to Puritan teaching, every soul was predestined by God from the beginning of time. This last teaching, together with the belief that God punishes every sin with sickness, sorrow, pain, or worse, appears to have caused terrible anxiety in Puritan children. One of many examples cited by historians is this entry in Reverend Samuel Sewall's diary, regarding his daughter Betty. He wrote:

When I came in past 7 at night, my wife met me in the entry and told me Betty [13 years old] had surprised

them. . . . It seems Betty had given some signs of dejection
and sorrow; a little after dinner, she burst out into an amaz-
ing cry which caused all the family to cry too; her mother
asked the reason; she gave none; at last she said she was
afraid she should go to hell, her sins were not pardoned. She
was first wounded by . . . a sermon. . . . The words . . . 'ye
shall seek me and shall die in your sins' ran in her mind and
terrified her greatly.

Perhaps Betty Parris and Abigail Williams were initially trauma-
tized by one of the Reverend Parris's sermons. Perhaps it was a com-
bination of fears. They had played with magic, for which God would
surely punish them. Since magic is related to the devil, perhaps they
thought he had power over them. Perhaps the girls thought it was the
devil who had caused the coffin to appear in the egg as a warning that
God would not pardon them, and they would go to hell.

★ In 1976 a graduate student named Linnda Caparael offered another
explanation of the Salem Village witchcraft crisis. She suggested that
an epidemic of food poisoning may have caused the widespread delusion. Eating bread made from rye grain contaminated with a fungus
could have caused ergotism, a condition causing symptoms similar to
those of the afflicted in Salem Village. Ergotism causes convulsions,
crawling sensations to the skin, dizziness, headaches, hallucinations,
muscle contractions, psychosis, delirium, vomiting, and diarrhea.

Ergotism might have brought on the first series of convulsions,
which Dr. Griggs diagnosed as witchcraft. But a victim of ergotism
whose condition is severe enough to bring on convulsions appears
thin, weak, and gray. Victims also suffer from severe intestinal pain,
something the girls rarely complained of. Nor is there any record of
the girls having suffered diarrhea.

The ergotism argument also overlooks the way the girls regularly
fell into convulsions whenever an accused person looked at them
with the "evil eye," or the way they came out of their fits and were
suddenly cured by the touch test. No one suffering from ergotism
has demonstrated an ability to start and stop convulsions seemingly
at will.

In the Hollywood movie The Wizard of Oz, *landowner Myra Gulch turns into the Wicked Witch of the West in Dorothy's dream. Some of the Salem women accused of witchcraft fit the Myra Gulch witch image.*

FEMINISTS AND WITCHCRAFT

"Mistress Hibbens was hanged for a witch only for having more wit than her neighbors."
—The Reverend John Norton

OF THE 20 PEOPLE EXECUTED AT SALEM, 14 WERE women. Twenty-five of the 31 people tried and convicted were women. One hundred four of the 141 people arrested were women. Most of these women were more than 40 years old. Among the charges brought against them were things such as "railing" in anger at a neighbor, cursing, muttering to themselves, persistently defending their property rights in court, generally behaving much like the fictional Myra Gulch in the 1939 Hollywood movie *The Wizard of Oz.* In the movie, Dorothy dreams that the bicycle-riding Myra Gulch turns into the Wicked Witch of the West. (Myra Gulch, by the way, is not in L. Frank Baum's book, on which the movie is loosely based.)

Sarah Good and Sarah Osborne fit the Myra Gulch witch image. Sarah Good had been robbed of her inheritance by her brother-in-law. She had fought him in court and won back a tiny portion of it, then lost it when her husband fell into debt. The marriage was apparently arranged by the people she worked for as a servant after her father's death. Though only in her late 30s at the time of her execution, Sarah

Good looked much older. Her matted hair, tobacco-stained teeth, ragged clothes, and hunched posture made her look like the hag witch of fairy tales.

Sarah Osborne, like Myra Gulch, was a fairly wealthy property owner. (Dorothy's Auntie Em says to Miss Gulch, "Just because you own half the county . . . ") A woman nearing 60 years of age, Sarah Osborne had long been entangled in a property dispute with her sons. She had also been at odds with her neighbors, apparently because of malicious gossip surrounding the workman who had lived in her house for two years before she married him.

Even Rebecca Nurse had "railed" at her neighbors when their pigs got into her vegetable garden. Yet she and her sister Mary Esty seemed more like martyrs than witches when they stood at the gallows. To those who watched them die, their grace and calm were profoundly

In the movie The Wizard of Oz, *Dorothy's Auntie Em, seated, says to Myra Gulch, "Just because you own half the county . . . "*

troubling, since they seemed to fulfill the Puritan ideal. (A third sister, Sarah Cloyce, was also accused, but she was not executed.)

In colonial Massachusetts, a witch by definition was the handmaid of the devil. To speak of good witches was to speak nonsense. Cotton Mather explained the apparent goodness in an accused witch. They used their magic to disguise themselves as martyrs, he said, even as the devil will sometimes don the robes of an angel of light. But even if witches were powerful enough to disguise themselves as saints, they were not powerful enough to save their own lives.

This powerlessness in a supposedly powerful figure, together with the Puritan image of the witch as woman—and woman as morally and intellectually weaker than man—has been a focal point for feminist historians. In interpreting witchcraft at Salem, feminist historians seek in part to understand the origin of some male prejudices women still face.

Historians have often cited property disputes between neighbors and family members as a major factor in the witchcraft trials. The focus of these arguments is generally on accusers versus those accused of witchcraft. Feminist historians, however, emphasize property lawsuits between men and women. Puritan religious ideals tended to categorize women into three groups: the young, virtuous, obedient daughter or maidservant; the submissive and supportive wife; and the discontented, greedy witch. Women who did not fit the first two categories tended to come under the close scrutiny of neighbors, who sometimes labeled them "witch."

Governor Winthrop tried to correct an early population imbalance by changing laws relating to female landowners. The first group of settlers to come to Massachusetts Bay Colony included a small number of married men, who had brought their wives with them, and a large number of unmarried men. To lure female settlers to the area, the governor passed a law in the 1630s granting "maid lotts" [parcels of land] to unmarried women. This law assured women the right to own property, but the land was also, in effect, a dowry—a gift to her future husband—since the community expected these women to marry. In 1640 another law was passed permitting husbands to will their property to their widows. The law also allowed fathers without sons to deed land to their daughters.

The lure worked. The female population grew, and many unmarried men took wives. By the 1650s, women outnumbered men in the Massachusetts Bay Colony. Many women owned property and operated farms and businesses in competition with their male neighbors. Disputes arose, especially after a husband died and left property to his widow. More and more frequently, the charge of witchcraft was leveled at women who had inherited property. Bridget Bishop and Susannah Martin had been accused of witchcraft shortly after their husbands had died and willed them property—prior to 1692. Their accusers were men whose property bordered theirs.

Though Bishop and Martin had both been acquitted of these early accusations, they were ever afterward plagued by the taunts of children and the slurs of neighbors who persisted in calling them "witch." By 1692 they were old, cranky, and mistrustful of magistrates. They fit the Myra Gulch, Wicked Witch of the West image portrayed in the *Wizard of Oz*. (The movie also had a Good Witch of the North, dressed in white and radiantly crowned.)

Belief in witches and witchcraft in Salem and Salem Village was based primarily on the writings of men. Puritan ministers and English judges published books defining witches and describing how to discover one. For example, Increase Mather wrote *Remarkable Provinces* in 1684. Many people doubted such writings and preferred not to prosecute women charged with witchcraft. This hesitation may explain why the witchcraft outbreak came so late in Salem. That it happened, however, was inevitable according to feminist historians. Even men who doubted whether a witch could be discovered and prosecuted believed that a woman who lusted after wealth, power, and knowledge—a woman who was discontent with her place in society—could be easily tempted by the devil.

Puritan ministers traced this "woman's weakness" back to Eve, the first woman God created, according to the Bible. Eve was tempted by a serpent in the garden of Eden. The serpent assured Eve that "In the day ye eat [of the forbidden fruit], your eyes shall be opened and ye

Puritan ministers connected women who wanted wealth, power, and knowledge to Eve, the first woman God created, according to the Bible. Eve gave in to the temptation of the devil—in the form of a serpent—and ate the forbidden fruit. She then convinced her husband, Adam, to do so.

shall be as gods." Eve "took of the fruit thereof, did eat, and gave also unto her husband; and he did eat." This Bible story was seen as an illustration not only of woman's inherent weakness in the face of temptation, but also of the corruption that befalls the man who is "ruled by his wife."

In Puritan society, marriage was an essential part of the ideal social order. Puritans believed that women were created for men so they might be wives and helpmates. In the home, the husband and father was the "godhead." As Christ rules the church and as the minister rules his congregation, so the good man must rule his household, the Puritans taught. The good wife was expected to be submissive, supportive, diligent, faithful, and pious. At the same time, her husband was expected to be faithful, pious, strong, wise, and loving. The husband who dealt too harshly with his wife was warned that such action could cause his wife to become discontent and easily tempted.

Discontent not only brought temptation to the unhappy wife, it also affected daughters and maidservants. The afflicted girls at Salem said that witches and the devil tempted them, offering them fine clothes, "pretty things," and even a husband. Their testimony reveals both a fear of and a yearning for the awesome power a witch was believed to wield.

Many Puritan girls believed that marriage was the only route to financial security. They also knew that the French and Indian wars seemed to be killing their hope. The coffin specter seen in the spinning egg may have seemed to confirm their worst fears. Young men and prosperous widowers were dying on the battlefield. Fathers and brothers had been killed defending home and hearth. Mercy Lewis and Sarah Churchill had witnessed their parents' brutal deaths during an attack by Native Americans. Indeed, of the 24 afflicted young people, 17 had lost one or both parents to war. More than half of these young people had become servants in the home of a relative or stranger.

Mary Warren illustrates the fine line between a "discontent woman" or "witch" and a "discontent maiden." The magistrates who summoned Warren to testify had assumed guilt in the cases of all the

Many Puritan girls thought marriage offered their only hope for financial security. This couple is on their way to church.

accused women. As the magistrates saw it, these women had already given in to temptation and served the devil, whereas the maidens who cried out against them, though tempted, struggled to resist. The fits they suffered demonstrated their struggles. Thus, when Mary Warren ceased to suffer, daring to say that she "did but dissemble," the magistrates assumed that she had given into temptation and signed the devil's book, since she no longer struggled to resist.

Mary Warren discovered the magistrates' view when she tried to testify in defense of John and Elizabeth Proctor. Sarah Churchill also tried to rescue George Jacobs and his wife by saying that she was only "distracted" and didn't know what she said when in her fits. Both girls were orphaned servants in the homes of those they briefly defended. When they saw that the magistrates seemed to turn on them, however, they became frightened and tumbled back into their fits to protect themselves.

Both the afflicted and the accused, most of whom were women, were at the mercy of male judges, sheriffs, advising ministers, and jury members. Two-thirds of the witnesses for the prosecution were male. Does this mean that the Salem witch-hunt was a male conspiracy? Not exactly, say many feminist historians. After all, the subservient role of women and a belief in witches was part of the Puritan culture—a culture born out of earlier Christian cultures carrying the same sentiments. True, the Puritan culture was largely shaped by the preaching and writing of men, and yes, men presided over witchcraft proceedings. Still, to call it a conspiracy is to miss the point.

According to some feminist interpretation, the power struggle between the court justices and the afflicted girls illustrates a desire for political and economic power among young women and male fear of powerful women—often thought of as witches. The Puritan man's patriarchal social order viewed discontented women, competitive business women, and prosperous women landowners as threats. There was no room for such women, unless they were seen as witches—intellectually and morally weak, physically and spiritually dangerous.

Historian Ann Kibbey of Yale University studied the letters and diaries of seventeenth-century Puritan men. She concluded that these

The Puritan religion placed a heavy responsibility on men, who felt they were responsible for the spiritual and physical well-being of family and servants.

men believed their thoughts and actions could influence nature through their link with God. The Puritan head of household apparently considered himself entirely responsible for the spiritual and physical well-being of his family and servants. When tragedy struck, he blamed himself, believing God had punished him because he had sinned. Samuel Sewall's statement of public repentance illustrates this belief. When two of his children died, he believed it was God's punishment for the role he had played in the witchcraft trials. Thus, God's wrath was seen as immediately linked—even controlled by— men's deeds.

Divine wrath and tests of faith included such woes as stormy weather, plagues of frogs and flies, sickness and death in the family, crop failure, sickness and death of farm animals, fire, accidents resulting in damage to people or property, the disappearance of objects, and every other conceivable mishap. These same misfortunes were often blamed on witchcraft as well. Divine wrath and witchcraft offered opposite explanations of the same events.

The Puritan head of household saw himself as standing in light, linked to God and all the powers of heaven—those powers weighing heavily against him when he sinned. At the same time, he saw the witch as a woman standing in darkness, linked to the devil—also with powers weighing against him. Witches, using the powers of the devil, could also cause storms, plagues, sickness, deaths, fires, and accidents.

The Puritan man who could no longer endure the weight of responsibility his religion placed on him looked for someone to blame. Thus the Reverend Parris threw off the burden of personal responsibility for the trouble in his household in 1692 and wrote a letter. Thomas Putnam, likewise, had troubles. He had lost every lawsuit he had brought against his neighbors. His wife had given birth to seven dead infants. Now his daughter and maidservant twisted in grotesque fits as if possessed by the devil. It was not his sin but some witch that brought this on him. He carried Reverend Parris's letter to the magistrates, a letter asking them to arrest three women. Accusing the women of witchcraft removed responsibility from the men. The witches, they said, were responsible for what had gone wrong.

In this scene from The Crucible, *the characters are,* from left
to right, *Mary Warren, John Proctor, and Mercy Lewis.
The play, by Arthur Miller, is based on the 1692 Salem
witch trials.*

SEVEN

A MODERN WITCH-HUNT

"The story of 1692 is of far more than antiquarian interest;
it is an allegory of our times."
—Marion Starkey, *Devil in Massachusetts*

I N 1952 ARTHUR MILLER'S PLAY *THE CRUCIBLE* WAS performed in Wilmington, New York. The play is set in Salem, Massachusetts in 1692. The hero, John Proctor, is depicted as a proud, honest, hardworking farmer in his thirties. He has committed adultery, which was a crime in Puritan society. If his act became public, his reputation—and the young woman's—would be ruined.

Abigail Williams, depicted in the play as a pretty, sensuous, 17-year-old, is the girl John Proctor seduced. She has lusted for him ever since their encounter. She even engaged in witchcraft rituals in an attempt to cause his wife's death. Abigail thought she could then marry John. But the Reverend Samuel Parris caught Abigail and her friends performing one of these rituals. As a result of the witchcraft, Betty Parris becomes sick. Her father sends for the Reverend John Hale who has had some experience with witchcraft cases.

When Hale arrives and questions Abigail, she blames Tituba. Hale then questions Tituba, who confesses to being a witch and practicing witchcraft. He urges her to name other witches. She names two—

Sarah Good and Sarah Osborne. Abigail and Betty catch on to the game and name others.

In the next scene, John Proctor's wife is arrested, having been accused by Abigail of being a witch. Proctor attempts to rescue her by presenting evidence that Abigail and the other girls are frauds and pretenders, but the court remains unconvinced. Even when he puts his reputation on the line and confesses his sin with Abigail, the judge refuses to release his wife. He suspects Proctor is attempting to overthrow the court. When Mary Warren cries out John Proctor's name, he, too, is arrested for witchcraft.

In the last scene of the play, ministers and magistrates meet with John Proctor in a squalid jail cell and urge him to confess. Because his reputation is already in shambles, he agrees to confess, reasoning that there can be little harm now in telling a lie to save his life. But

This scene from The Crucible *shows actors portraying,* from left to right, *Betty Parris, Susanna Wallcott, Mercy Lewis, Abigail Williams, Mary Warren, and Deputy Governor Danfort.*

the judge wants more. He asks Proctor to name other witches and wizards and to sign a written confession so the court can advertise his compliance. He refuses and is led off stage. A drum roll signals his execution.

At its first performance, *The Crucible* received thunderous applause and calls for the author to take a bow. Everyone in the audience had read in newspapers or heard on the radio about a new kind of witch-hunt. The accusation this time was not witchcraft, but Communism.

In 1938, the House Committee on Un-American Activities (HUAC), a congressional committee, was set up as a special investigating committee with the goal of protecting the U.S. government from Communist infiltration. The committee accused many Americans of membership in the Communist Party. The only way to escape punishment was to confess to previous Communist activities, repent, renounce those activities, and name fellow Communists.

The committee's critics charged that it often abused its investigative power and violated the constitutional rights of witnesses. They maintained that people labeled as subversives should have the right to cross-examine their accusers. HUAC had admitted speculative evidence (theoretical evidence that could not be demonstrated), just as the Court of Oyer and Terminer had admitted spectral evidence. The committee also presumed guilt in those who stood accused, just as the judges had at Salem.

Senator Joseph McCarthy of Wisconsin made widespread accusations and led investigations of people, organizations, and government agencies suspected of Communist activities or even Communist sympathy. Government workers, librarians, public officials, college professors, writers, entertainers, and people in many other professions became suspect, usually with little or no evidence against them. Many businesses blacklisted (refused to hire) people accused of associating with Communists, even if there was no proof. Many employees were required to take oaths of loyalty to the U.S. government. McCarthy and members of his committee also encouraged the accused to supply names of other people whom they thought *might* be

Senator Joseph McCarthy, in foreground, *conducted a witch-hunt of his own, but he was looking for Communists instead of witches.*

associated with the Communist Party. The HUAC hearings bore a strange resemblance to the Salem witch trials, and Miller's play portrayed that similarity.

Not everyone, however, appreciated the comparison Miller's play made between witchcraft in Salem Village in 1692 and anti-Communist hysteria in 1952. During some performances of the play, a sheet of ice seemed to form over the audience. The objection Miller heard over and over again was that Communists were real, witches were not.

One 1953 performance became a spontaneous memorial service. After Proctor had been led offstage to be executed, the audience stood with bowed heads during the drum roll, as if in silent prayer. Earlier that day, Julius and Ethel Rosenberg, two American civilians, had been executed in the electric chair for spying for the Soviet Union during World War II. They had been accused of passing secret information about the manufacture of the atom bomb to the Soviets. They

Ethel and Julius Rosenberg were convicted of giving secret atomic-bomb information to the Soviet Union during World War II. They maintained their innocence until their execution in Sing Sing prison on June 19, 1953.

pleaded innocent, but in 1951 a jury found the Rosenbergs guilty of conspiracy to commit espionage, and Judge Irving Kaufman sentenced them to death. Protesters in the United States and Europe organized in opposition to the conviction and sentence. Many people felt that the Rosenbergs had not gotten a fair trial and that their sentence was too harsh. Even the great scientist Albert Einstein and Pope Pius XII urged clemency. The case was appealed to the Supreme Court, but the Court denied all appeals. President Dwight Eisenhower twice denied pleas for clemency. The Rosenbergs were executed in 1953 at Sing Sing prison in Ossining, New York.

Their execution had an unsettling effect, as did the executions of 1692. Politicians, ministers, and judges had debated the wisdom of allowing spectral evidence in court proceedings after the 1692 trials and hangings. In 1953, politicians and members of the press questioned

The Communist Party

In 1917, Russia became the first state to be controlled by the Communist Party. During the following years, other territories joined Russia to form the Union of Soviet Socialist Republics (U.S.S.R.), also known as the Soviet Union. After World War II (1939–1945), Soviet troops occupied many countries in Eastern Europe and set up Communist governments there. The Soviet Union became one of the most powerful countries in the world.

The term *communism* has several meanings. It can be an economic system, a form of government, a way of life, or a goal or ideal. The Communism of the Soviet Union was based on a set of ideas taken from the writing of Karl Marx, a German philosopher. Marx's ideas were developed in Russia by Vladimir Lenin, a revolutionary leader in the early 1900s. Communism calls for government ownership (rather than private ownership) of land, businesses, housing, and schools. The government imposed strict rule by the Communist Party, which affected all aspects of people's lives. To take power and impose its rule, the Communist Party often used force without regard to law.

The rapid spread of Communism brought about a struggle for power and influence between Communist and non-Communist countries throughout the world. This struggle became known as the Cold War. During this period, the United States and the Soviet Union were bitter enemies. The Soviets threatened to take over the world. Governments of the free world wanted to limit Soviet influence.

Finally, during the late 1980s and the early 1990s the Cold War came to an end, and the Soviet Union collapsed. After 1992, only a few countries remained under Communist rule.

HUAC's use of speculative evidence. Evidence against Ethel Rosenberg appeared weak at best. By condemning and executing both husband and wife, the state had orphaned their two school-age children.

Arthur Miller was not the first author to note the parallel between witchcraft hysteria in 1692 and the anti-Communist mood in the 1940s and 1950s. Marion Starkey's book, *The Devil in Massachusetts*, triggered playwright Miller's imagination. Her narrative history, rich with colorful descriptions, applies the psychological theories of Janet and Freud in a context of Cold War metaphors.

For Arthur Miller, those metaphors reflected personal experience. The same weekend he went to Salem to research the witchcraft cases, he stopped to visit a close friend. Miller's friend told him he had given in to HUAC's demands. The friend had served as an informer, much like Margaret Jacobs, who had confessed to being a witch and later testified against her grandfather in the hope of avoiding the gallows herself. Miller's friend wanted to avoid being blacklisted.

Playwright Arthur Miller, right, *testifies before the House Committee on Un-American Activities (HUAC) in 1956.*

Four years later, Miller himself was summoned to appear before HUAC. The committee presented as evidence a stack of petitions and statements Miller had signed during the 1920s and 1930s, when many young intellectuals tended to view Communist ideology as an ethical solution to political and social problems. When Arthur Miller appeared before HUAC in 1956, he "confessed" to having had Communist sympathies as a young man, and he "repented," saying he had long since renounced Communism. But the committee wanted more. Arthur Miller, like the John Proctor in *The Crucible,* was asked to name other offenders. Miller refused and was charged with contempt of court. (The charges were later dropped, and he did not go to prison.)

In 1954 *The Crucible* became an off-Broadway hit in New York City. Critics raved, saying the author must have revised it. He had not. The political atmosphere, however, had changed. Senator Joseph McCarthy, the Cotton Mather of the 1940s and early 1950s, was censured—given a condemning judgment—by the Senate in 1954.

Like the Court of Oyer and Terminer, the HUAC hearings destroyed the lives of many innocent people. Both McCarthy and Mather had political gain in mind when each man loudly supported the legal proceedings of his day. Mather preached from horseback, from the pulpit, and through his books. McCarthy preached in front of the press, on the radio, and in newspaper headlines. Both men were respected and well known. Both men fell from power because of their own words. Cotton Mather was warned by friends, and perhaps even by his father, that it would be prudent to publicly question the court's use of spectral evidence. Instead, he gave full support to all court proceedings.

Fellow Republicans likewise warned McCarthy about carrying the Communist issue too far. Instead of heeding the warning, McCarthy accused the U.S. Army of "coddling Communists." The army brought countercharges of improper conduct against members of McCarthy's staff. The army appointed attorney Joseph Welch to defend its reputation in court. He used McCarthy's own words against him, just as Robert Calef had used Cotton Mather's own words against him when writing *More Wonders of the Invisible World.* As a result of the hearings, McCarthy lost the support of millions of people, and his political and personal life crumbled.

Cotton Mather never realized his political hopes either. At a time when he might have been president of Harvard College and an influential member of the Massachusetts Council, he found himself shunned and mocked, even by his grandchildren.

McCarthyism, like the Salem witchcraft hysteria, came and went. Yet *The Crucible* lives on as Miller's most frequently produced play worldwide. Through it, the Salem witchcraft trials became a symbol not just of McCarthyism, but of any governmental policy based on fear, ignorance, and abuse of power. Miller wrote, "I can almost tell what the political situation in a country is when it *[The Crucible]* is suddenly a hit there."

The Salem Witch Museum in Salem, Massachusetts

── ⚜ EIGHT ⚜ ──

WITCH CITY

"People are not passive victims of historical change, but active participants."
—Larry Gragg, *The Salem Witch Crisis*

THE CONTEMPORARY HISTORIAN VISITING SALEM, Massachusetts, will discover a localized, commercial interpretation of the history of witchcraft. Visitors are invited to "stop by for a spell" at "the bewitched seaport." Among the attractions are the Witch Dungeon Museum and a *History Alive!* performance at the Old Town Hall.

At Witch Dungeon Museum, performers reenact segments of the witchcraft trials in a fictionalized presentation. Actors speak directly to people in the audience, appealing to them as though they were period spectators who might sway the opinion of the court. The accused pleads her innocence, the accuser screams "guilty!" Feelings of terror and confusion are vividly portrayed, and people in the audience are drawn into the drama, as they were in 1692.

Following the reenactment, guides lead the audience on a tour of a replica of the Salem prison. The exhibit is in a dark, dank setting, and mannequin prisoners in period costumes exude a spooky sadness.

At Old Town Hall, actors portray the trial of Bridget Bishop in a drama called *Cry Innocent: The People vs. Bridget Bishop.* The script uses original dialogue and testimony, as recorded in court documents of 1692. The audience participates, serving as members of the jury. After hearing all the evidence for and against Bridget, the audience is invited to condemn or acquit her.

Why do the people of Salem perform reenactments of so notorious and brief a segment of their history? Because tourists want to see it. Unable to escape its past, Salem has slowly given in to ever growing tourist demands for witch-related souvenirs, exhibits, and performances. As early as the 1830s, visitors hiked along Gallows Hill, also known as Witch Hill. The visitors picked and carried home rare wildflowers in the belief that they might possess magical or medicinal properties. About 40 years later, visitors could purchase a painted pebble, depicting a witch flying over Salem on a broomstick. It was the first witch souvenir marketed in Salem. Seeing how popular these pebbles were, a few astute businesspeople exploited the witch logo. Around 1888, one company manufactured and sold silver collectors' spoons with the witch logo on them. The same company later offered jewelry and tea strainers with the witch logo.

In 1892, as a bicentennial commemorative of the Salem witch trials, another merchant produced collector plates that profiled the witch as a Greek goddess. This romanticized image did not last, however.

Visitors to Salem will find that the logo of a witch on a broomstick decorates police and fire department uniforms and vehicles. It also appears on newspaper boxes, at the masthead of the *Salem Evening Post*, on storefronts and postcards. A witch is the mascot for the Salem High School football team. It even inspired Witch's Brew ale and the popular ice-cream flavor, Salem Witch Sludge.

Souvenirs abound. Museum gift shops sell witch-related books, videos, mugs, T-shirts, key rings, pencils, hats, brooms, and Halloween decor. In addition to the Witch Dungeon Museum, Salem Witch Museum, Witch House, the Salem Wax Museum of Witches and Seafarers, and the House of Seven Gables also welcome visitors.

The House of Seven Gables is the site of the earliest known souvenir shop in the area. "Hepzibah's Shop," a store named after a character in Nathaniel Hawthorne's famous novel *House of Seven Gables*, first sold painted pebbles and collector china to tourists. In the early 1900s, the same shop sold the first Halloween witch postcards depicting a fun-loving witch who looked like Mother Goose.

In those days, visitors to Salem were relatively few, and those who did come were generally from neighboring New England cities and states. Increased interest has led to a million or so tourists tromping through "Witch City" every year. The largest concentration comes during Salem's Halloween Octoberfest of Haunted Happenings. What caused this flood tide of tourists? Marion Starkey's book, Arthur Miller's play, a Hollywood movie, and a television miniseries based on the Salem witchcraft trials each heightened popular interest. Meanwhile, long-distance travel became easy and affordable. People come from Japan, South America, Europe, and all parts of the United States to learn about the happenings that took place in late-seventeenth-century Salem.

Author Nathaniel Hawthorne, right, *was a descendant of John Hathorne, one of the justices at the Salem witch trials. Hawthorne changed his name to disassociate himself from the behavior of his ancestor. The House of Seven Gables is below.*

At first, there was not much to see at Salem. Visitors could tour "Witch House," the former residence of Judge Jonathan Corwin, or see the House of Seven Gables. They could hike over Witch Hill, also called Gallows Hill, or search for the gravestone of Judge John Hathorne. For a short time in the mid-1960s, visitors could even peer at the ruins of the old Salem dungeon, where some of those accused of witchcraft were said to have been imprisoned. Construction workers uncovered the dungeon while tearing down an old building, but it was soon dismantled and used for landfill. Only two beams survive. One is in the Peabody Museum at Salem. The other was built into the replica prison at Witch Dungeon Museum.

Salem tourists often ask where the witches were burned. Hoping to correct this misconception, and at the same time satisfy growing tourist demands for witch-related media, Holly Mulvahill Lynch founded Salem Witch Museum. Housed in a hundred-year-old former Unitarian church, the neo-Gothic museum opened in 1970. That same year, ABC-TV aired the "Salem Saga" episode of the popular television show *Bewitched*.

Salem Witch Museum uses life-sized dioramas—scenic representations with sculptured figures and realistically painted backgrounds—and dramatic light and sound effects to depict the key events of 1692. The first illuminated image is that of a horned, winged devil, which represents the darkest colonial witchcraft beliefs and fears. A brief, legendary history follows, depicting Abigail Williams's alleged boredom, Betty Parris's supposed sickness, Tituba's fireside stories, Rebecca Nurse's trial, John Proctor's stubbornness and subsequent arrest, and George Burrough's hanging.

These scenes reflect Marion Starkey's history and Arthur Miller's characterizations. The last scene shows Ann Putnam Jr. confessing to having been deluded by the devil when she accused innocent Christians of being witches. The museum narrator then closes on an upbeat note, emphasizing the speed with which Salem's forefathers recognized and repented of their errors and expressing the hope that all other racial, religious, and political injustices might end as quickly.

This diorama at the Salem Witch Museum shows Tituba, right, *with Betty Parris and Abigail Williams.*

About five years after the Salem Witch Museum opened, the people of Salem were challenged to prove their lack of prejudice toward witches. Laurie Cabot, a self-proclaimed witch, moved into town. She opened Crow Haven Corner, a shop nestled in an old townhouse across the street from the Essex Institute, where the original documents pertaining to the Salem witchcraft trials are kept. Shoppers at Cabot's store can buy incense, herbs, crystals, candles, pendants, charms, and other Wicca witch products.

Laurie Cabot not only opened a witch shop in Salem, she began to dress like a witch as an outward expression of her beliefs. Her hair is wild and carefree, her robe long and black, her hands adorned with rings. Around her neck, she wears a pentagram pendant, a five-pointed star. Laurie does not wear a tall pointed hat, nor does she ride—or even carry—a broom. In fact, she has frequently protested Salem's logo of a witch on a broomstick. She says it misrepresents witches. Witches, she insists, are not ugly old women, and they certainly don't fly through the air on broomsticks. They do not practice black magic, nor do they have anything to do with the devil or Satanic rites. Despite these assertions, some people shield their eyes

Laurie Cabot, a self-proclaimed witch, opened a shop in Salem, Massachusetts.

when they pass Laurie Cabot on the street. They are afraid she will give them the "evil eye."

Most people in Salem are not afraid of Laurie Cabot, however. Mention of her produces smiles, shrugs, and head shaking. Yet these same people admit they were offended when Massachusetts governor Michael Dukakis bestowed on Laurie the title Official Witch of Salem in the late 1980s, an honor the city mayor—with the support of the people—had refused to grant.

Laurie Cabot's presence has turned out to be a commercial boon to Salem. Besides producing greater tourist interest, she has also attracted other witches. Those who practice modern witchcraft say that their craft has nothing to do with the devil or black magic (although devil cults still exist, and voodoo and black magic are still practiced in some corners of the world). Modern Wicca witches worship Mother Earth—goddess of fertility, life, and nourishment. They believe their magic lies in their power to join themselves spiritually with Mother Earth, with all of nature, and with each other through the practice of meditation. They believe this spiritual bond with nature and their goddess can actually have a physical influence on such things as weather and health.

Wicca witches come by the hundreds every Halloween. On Halloween night, they walk in a candlelight procession, wearing robes and chanting. The witches gather around the Salem Witchcraft Trial Memorial as part of their ritual. The memorial was completed in 1992, the tercentennial (300th anniversary) of the Salem witchcraft trials. Nobel Peace Prize winner Elie Wiesel, a Nazi concentration camp survivor, dedicated the monument. Arthur Miller and many

The Salem Witch Trials Memorial in Salem, Massachusetts

Salem witchcraft historians attended the ceremony. Snuggled against Old Burying Point, where Magistrate John Hathorne is buried, the memorial is a wide, low, open-ended rectangular wall of rough-hewn granite. Twenty stone benchmarks protrude along the inside of the wall, each etched with the name of one of those executed during the trials, including Giles Corey. The words of the executed, protesting their innocence, are carved into the wall.

To many viewers, the memorial has a certain sanctity. It represents religious zeal at its best—and at its worst. It represents those who clung to truth and died like martyrs and those who condemned their neighbors on the basis of fear, greed, and ignorance. The low, heavy, rough-edged monument reminds people of both human frailty and human strength. That so sacred a place should be incorporated into Wicca rituals has upset some people.

To Wicca witches, Halloween is Samhain, a holy day marking the end of the harvest and the beginning of winter. Samhain is an ancient Celtic festival. The Celts, who have lived for more than 2,000 years in what is now Great Britain, Ireland, and coastal France, were pagan before they converted to Christianity in A.D. 300 Their pagan New Year began on November 1. On October 31, their New Year's Eve, they held a festival in honor of Samhain, the Celtic lord of death. The celebration marked the beginning of the season of cold, darkness, and decay, which they associated with human death. The Celts believed that Samhain allowed the souls of those who had died that year to return to their earthly homes before rising into the spirit realm.

On the evening of the festival, the druids—the priests and teachers of the Celts—ordered the people to put out their hearth fires. The druids then built a huge New Year's bonfire of oak branches, which they considered sacred. They burned harvest offerings, such as animals and crops. Some archaeologists think they may have also offered human sacrifices. After the festival, each family carried a torch home and relit its hearth fire from the New Year's fire. Christians later incorporated part of this pagan festival into their own tradition, lighting candles and praying for the souls of the dead on Halloween—All Hallows' Eve—the night before All Saints' Day.

Wiccan priestess Selena Fox, right, is the founder and director of Circle Sanctuary, the first legally established Wiccan church in the United States. Wiccans worship Mother Earth—goddess of fertility, life, and nourishment—in her many forms, left.

Wicca witches incorporated the Salem memorial into their Samhain ritual as a way of expressing deep gratitude. They can safely express their beliefs in Salem, in part because of the sacrifice those 20 people made in 1692. Selena Fox, a Wiccan priestess, is founder and executive director of Circle Sanctuary, one of the first legally established Wiccan churches in the United States. According to Fox, "Three hundred years after the Salem trials, Wiccan witches are still struggling for their rights as a religious and cultural minority in American society." The battles are taking place in the courts, in state legislatures, and in the media. Fox said, "I hope that as present and future generations reflect on the lessons of Salem, that we will all work together for a society that celebrates diversity and truly offers freedom for all."

The original witchcraft deposition, or testimony. It includes the names of Samuel Parris, Nathaniel Ingersoll, and Thomas Putnam. The deposition, dated 30 April 1692, is signed by John Hathorne and Jonathan Corwin.

BECOMING A HISTORIAN

HISTORIANS ARE A LITTLE BIT LIKE UNDERCOVER agents. They learn about something that happened, then try to figure out who did it and why. Historians are also experts. When a major event occurs, such as the collapse of the Soviet Union, news reporters call the "experts" and ask, "Why is this happening? What can you tell us that would help people understand this event?" The experts almost always talk about history, because they know that what happened a long time ago often affects current events.

How does someone become an expert? In part, by studying and doing research. For the historian, research is like treasure hunting. One historian who was studying the Salem trials lived in an old, historic house in Danvers (which used to be Salem Village). He did some of his research in the cellar of his house. He dug in the dirt floor to find any artifacts that might have been left there. He also spent long hours at a church, reading letters and sermon notes written by the Reverend Samuel Parris. In order to better understand the treasures he found, he went to the library and checked out books about Salem history.

How does a beginning historian get started? First, find out what

Some artifacts excavated from the cellar of a house in Danvers,
Massachusetts—formerly Salem Village

other historians have written about the subject. Visit the library, ask the reference librarian to help you find bibliographical information. A bibliography is a written record of books, manuscripts, and articles. It tells people what sources an author used when he or she was doing research.

Besides reading, you might also consider traveling to historic sites and visiting museums. Talk to reenactment historians and museum curators. Write to a historian who knows the subject you want to research.

Along the way, take notes and keep a record of all your sources. This step is crucial. One has to get the facts right before interpreting them. When interpreting history, you might want to look at current issues and compare them to past events. Arthur Miller, for example, compared the Salem witchcraft trials to the McCarthy hearings.

Historians use two kinds of sources, primary and secondary. Primary sources are firsthand accounts and original records (or reproductions of the same). Secondary sources are books and articles written by later historians. This book is a secondary source.

Early histories, such as those written by Deodat Lawson or Cotton Mather, are primary sources. They have no bibliographies. In those days, the integrity of the writer was based on his or her reputation. If the author was known to be an honest person, then the work was accepted as true—that is until someone like Robert Calef published a challenge.

How much information is in a bibliography? Books are listed by author, title, place of publication, publisher, and copyright date. Articles are listed by author, title of article, name of the magazine or journal, date of publication, and the page numbers on which the article is printed. Manuscripts and other original sources are listed by author, title (if there is one), approximate date, and the name of the library or institution in which it is located.

To write this book, I used the books listed under Sources of Information. Can you match the source with the chapter?

SOURCES OF INFORMATION

Narratives of the Witchcraft Cases. Introduction and notes by George L. Burr. New York: Barnes & Noble, 1972. This book contains the collected reprints of works by Increase Mather, Samuel Willard, Cotton Mather, Deodat Lawson, John Hale, and Robert Calef, plus letters by Governor Phips, and Thomas Brattle related to the witchcraft trials at Salem.

The Salem Witchcraft Papers. Edited by Paul Boyer and Stephen Nissenbaum. New York: Works Progress Administration, 1977. The book is a reprint of the original court records, with introduction by the editors.

Sewall, Samuel. *Diary of Samuel Sewall, 1674–1708.* Reprinted with notes and chronology by M. Halsey Thomas. New York: Farrar Straus & Giroux, 1973.

The following secondary sources were also used:

Breslaw, Elaine G. *Tituba:* Reluctant Witch of Salem. New York: New York University Press, 1996.

Cabot, Laurie. *Power of the Witch.* New York: Bantam Doubleday Dell Publishers, 1989.

Caporael, Linnda R. "Ergotism: The Satan Loosed in Salem?" *Science* 192 (1976): 21–46.

Caulfield, Ernest. "Pediatric Aspects of the Salem Witchcraft Tragedy: A Lesson in Mental Health." *American Journal of Diseases of Children* 65 (1943): 788–802.

Demos, John Putnam. *Entertaining Satan: Witchcraft and the Culture of Early New England.* Oxford: Oxford University Press, 1982. This book presents a demographical, psychological, and sociological analysis of Salem witchcraft.

Freud, Sigmund. *The Origin and Development of Psychoanalysis,* vol. 54 of Great Books Series. Chicago: Encyclopedia Britannica, Inc., 1952.

Fried, Richard. *Nightmare in Red: The McCarthy Era in Perspective.* Oxford: Oxford University Press, 1990.

Gragg, Larry Dale. *The Salem Witch Crisis.* New York: Praeger, 1992. Although this is a secondary source, it reflects the author's thorough knowledge of rare primary sources written by the Reverend Samuel Parris.

Hansen, Chadwick. *Witchcraft at Salem.* New York: George Braziller Publications, 1969. This book draws on the research and lectures of Jean Charcot and Pierre Janet in interpreting the witchcraft affliction in Salem Village. It concludes that some of those hanged were guilty of practicing black magic.

Karlsen, Carol F. *The Devil in the Shape of a Woman: Witchcraft in Colonial New England.* New York: W. W. Norton and Co., 1987.

Kibbey, Ann. "The Mutation of the Supernational: Witchcraft, Remarkable Providences, and the Power of Puritan Men," *American Quarterly* 34: 125–48.

Laming, Annette. *Lascaux Paintings and Engravings.* Translated by Eleanore Armstrong. New York: Penguin Books, 1959.

Miller, Arthur. *The Crucible.* New York: Bantam Books, 1959.

———. *Timebends: An Autobiography.* New York: Grove Press, 1987.

The Riverside Anthology of Children's Literature. Edited by Judith Saltman. Boston: Houghton Mifflin, 1985.

Rosenthal, Bernard. *Salem Story: Reading the Witch Trials of 1692.* Cambridge: Cambridge University Press, 1993. This book takes an analytical approach to the subject. The last chapter talks about modern Salem and the effect history has had on the city.

Seligmann, Kurt. *Magic, Supernaturalism and Religion.* New York: Pantheon Books, 1948.

Starkey, Marion. *The Devil in Massachusetts.* New York: Alfred A. Knopf, 1949.

Summers, Montague. *The Geography of Witchcraft.* London: Trench Trubner & Co., 1927.

Wendell, Barrett. "Were the Salem Witches Guiltless?" *Essex Institute Historical Collections* 29 (1892): 129–47. This compares the behavior of nineteenth-century occult mediums to that of the afflicted people at Salem Village in 1692.

Williams, Selma, and Pamela Williams. *Riding the Nightmare: Women and Witchcraft.* New York: Atheneum, 1978.

INDEX

About the Author: Lori Lee Wilson received her B. A. in history at Westmont College in California in 1977. Since then, she has written for magazines and newspapers. She also won an Award of Merit from a branch of the Vermont Historical Society for her book length bicentennial history of Trinity Episcopal Church in Shelburne, Vermont. This is her first book with Lerner.

Lori's love of history is due in part to the stories her mother, grandmothers, and great-grandmother told her in response to the questions she was forever asking them. "I was hungry for knowledge and fascinated by the fact that the adventures my mother and grandparents told me really happened." She has since discovered that her own children are equally fascinated by "true stories."

Illustration Acknowledgments: American Antiquarian Society, 62; Archive Photos, 8, 9, 12 (center), 13 (both), 26, 27, 32 (left), 54, 66, 79, 82, 88, 89, 97; The Bettmann Archive, 2-3, 6, 12 (left and right), 14 (right), 16, 39, 48 (left), 50, 55, 97 (inset); Circle Sanctuary Archive, 103 (right); Corbis-Bettmann 14 (left), 48 (right), 56, 65, 67; Danvers Archival Center 18, 31, 40, 44, 46, 52, 59; Essex Institute, 61; Selena Fox, 103 (left); Hollywood Book and Poster, 74; IPS, 70; Library of Congress, 19, 80; Massachusetts Historical Society, 24; Rebecca Nurse Homestead, 57; Courtesy of the Peabody Essex Museum, Salem, Massachusetts, 32 (right), 34, 38, 69, 72, 104; Photofest, 10, 76, 84, 86; Henry W. Rutkowski, 71; Salem Office of Tourism and Cultural Affairs, 100; Salem Witch Museum, 35, 42, 43, 49, 94, 99, 101 (both); Richard B. Trask, 106; UPI/Corbis-Bettmann, 91.